NOTTINGHAM
- LONG EATON -
DERBY

Vic Mitchell & Keith Smith

MP Middleton Press

Front cover: Class 8F 2-8-0 no. 48149 passes through Draycott & Breaston in about 1950. (Colour-Rail.com)

Back cover: Railway Clearing House map for 1947 (edited). The key indicates ownership at that time.

Published February 2020
First reprint December 2021
Second reprint May 2022
Third reprint April 2023

ISBN 978 1 910356 43 2

© Middleton Press Ltd, 2020

Production Editor & Cover design Deborah Esher
Typesetting & Design Cassandra Morgan

Published by
　　Middleton Press Ltd
　　Camelsdale Road
　　Haslemere
　　Surrey
　　GU27 3RJ
Tel: 01730 813169
Email: info@middletonpress.co.uk
www.middletonpress.co.uk

Printed by 4Bind Ltd, Unit B Caxton Point, Caxton Way, Stevenage, Hertfordshire SG1 2XU
Telephone +44 (0) 1438 745005; www.4bind.co.uk

CONTENTS

ACKNOWLEDGEMENTS

We are very grateful for the assistance received from many of those mentioned in the credits, also from A.J.Castledine, G.Croughton, G.Gartside, J.Hinson (Signalling Record Society), C.M.Howard, N.Langridge, B.Lewis, D. and Dr S. Salter and, in particular, our always supportive families.

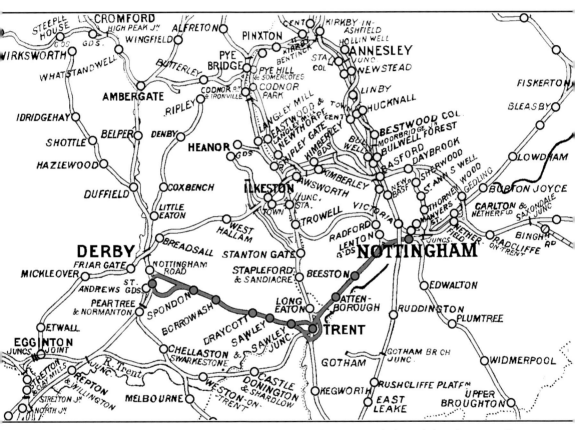

I. The 1947 Railway Clearing House edition has the album route darkened, but the name 'Long Eaton' was applied to Sawley Junction instead from 1968.

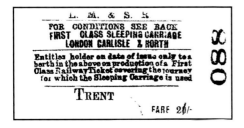

GEOGRAPHICAL SETTING

The route was built in the counties of Derbyshire and Nottinghamshire, their boundary being crossed one mile southwest of Attenborough. Our journey is within a mile of the River Trent from Nottingham to Trent Junction and thereafter is close to the winding River Derwent, to Derby.

The underlying geology of the line consists of mainly red sandstones. The valuable coal fields were to be found north and south of the route.

There were canals and/or navigable rivers in four directions from Long Eaton prior to the advent of the railways, but the latter were soon able to provide closer services.

The maps are to the scale of 25ins to 1 mile, with north at the top, unless otherwise indicated.

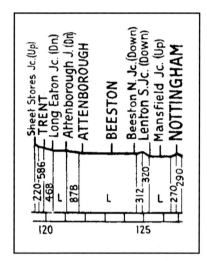 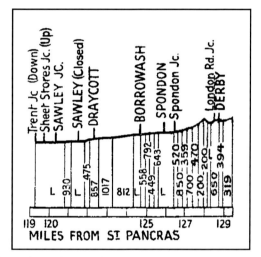

For reasons unknown, the early engineers chose to record their gradient profiles in opposite directions from Trent.

HISTORICAL BACKGROUND

The Midland Counties Railway came into action between Derby and Nottingham on 4th June 1839, the former was reached by an extension of the London & Birmingham Railway on 12th August 1839. The MCR opened a line southwards from the Trent area in 1840. (The station name changes are detailed later, at Trent.) This branch reached Rugby on 30th June 1840. A direct link from there to London came in 1857.

The above routes became a part of the Midland Railway on 11th May 1844. In 1847, it extended the line north from Trent to Chesterfield and beyond. Its extension east from Nottingham to Lincoln opened on 4th August 1846.

An MR line north from Nottingham reached Radford and beyond to Mansfield in 1848. A branch from there westward to Trowell was completed in 1875. The north-south route through the centre of Nottingham was completed in 1899 by the Great Central Railway. It closed to passengers in 1969 and entirely in 1974. The MR provided a line to Nottingham from Melton Mowbray in 1879, but it was closed in 1968.

The MR had become part of the London Midland & Scottish Railway in 1923 and the GCR then became a constituent of the London & North Eastern Railway. Upon nationalisation in 1948, most of the LMSR formed the London Midland Region of British Railways, while much of the LNER became its Eastern Region. On 2nd April 1950, all former LMSR lines north and east of Hasland, Dore & Totley, Sheffield and Barnsley were moved to the Eastern Region.

Following privatisation, main line services from London St Pancras towards Nottingham and Derby were operated by Midland Mainline (owned by National Express) from 28th April 1996 until 10th November 2007. Local and regional services in the area were operated by Central Trains (also owned by National Express) between 2nd March 1997 and 10th November 2007. From 11th November 2007, MML services were amalgamated into the new East Midlands Trains franchise (owned by Stagecoach). The Central Trains franchise was split, with some services also becoming part of EMT and others merged into the new CrossCountry franchise (owned by Arriva) on the same day. EMT services transferred to a new East Midlands Railway (EMR) franchise on 18th August 2019. This is owned by Abellio.

PASSENGER SERVICES

The table gives sample figures for trains running on at least five days per week. In the steam era, many of the journey opportunities shown below involved changing at Trent, which acted as the 'cross roads' for the district. Not shown are the stopping trains from the south, from Leicester to Nottingham.

	Fast		Stopping	
	Weekdays	Sundays	Weekdays	Sundays
1842	1	1	4	2
1873	12	3	8	3
1901	17	9	10	3
1921	15	8	8	4
1951	7	9	8	0
1981	7	0	11	11

Until 2007, MML operated a 2 trains per hour service between Trent Junction and Nottingham. There was also a similar service between Trent Junction and Derby, one of which extended to Sheffield. Some trains were extended to Scarborough, Leeds or Barnsley. Under EMT from December 2009, both Derby trains ran to Sheffield. EMT also operated hourly local services: Newark Castle to Matlock, across the whole route, and Lincoln Central to Leicester, between Nottingham and Trent Junction. EMR has continued this pattern since it began operations. CrossCountry also ran services across the whole route twice an hour: one from Nottingham to Birmingham New Street, while one extended to Cardiff Central.

Bradshaw's timetable for 1st January 1845.

Hotel advertisements from *Good Lines*, monthly journal of the Temperance Society, dated 1911.

DERBY, TRENT, NOTTINGHAM, SOUTHWELL, NEWARK, and LINCOLN.—Midland.

Mls	Fares 1 cl.	2 cl.	3 cl.	Fm M'chester, 184.	mrn	mail	mrn	mrn	mrn	mrn	mrn	mrn	mrn	mrn	aft	aft	aft	aft	aft	aft	aft	aft	aft	aft	aft (Mondays, Fridays, & Saturdays only.)	Sundays. mrn	mail	mrn	mrn	aft	aft	aft
				Derby (Sta. St.) d	1 0	3 16	6 15	6 50	7 40	8 38	9c0	9 30	1020	1135	1235	1c0	2 30	3 10	4c15	5 15	5 20	6 15	6 40	8c20	....	1 0	3 16	6 50	8 45	6 33	7 25	8c0
2¾	0 6	0 4	0 2½	Spondon	....	....	....	6 58	7 46	....	9 8	....	1026	....	....	1 6	2 36	....	4 23	....	5 28	6 24	....	8 27	....	....	....	6 57	8 52	....	7 31	8 7
4½	0 8	0 5	0 4	Borrowash	....	....	....	7 3	7 51	....	9 13	....	1031	....	....	1 11	2 40	....	4 28	....	5 33	6 28	....	8 32	....	....	....	7 2	8 57	....	7 36	8 12
6½	1 0	0 8	0 6	Draycott	....	....	....	7 10	7 57	....	9 19	....	1037	....	....	1 17	2 46	....	4 33	....	5 39	6 34	....	8 38	....	....	....	7 9	9 2	....	7 41	8 18
7½	1 0	0 9	0 6	Sawley	....	....	....	7 14	....	....	9 22	....	1041	....	....	....	2 49	....	4 36	....	5 43	6 38	....	8 42	....	....	....	7 13	9 6	....	7 45	8 22
9½	1 6	1 3	0 8	Trent 190 arr	1 16	....	6 32	7 23	8 6	8 55	9 27	9 50	1047	1152	1252	1 24	2 55	3 27	4 45	5 32	5 49	6 45	6 57	8 48	....	1 16	....	7 19	....	6 47	7 53	....
				Trent 190 dep	1 25	....	6 40	7 27	8 9	9 5	9 29	9 58	1055	12 4	1256	1 25	3 0	3 36	4 47	5 35	5 55	6 47	7 10	8 50	....	1 25	....	....	9 13	7 0	....	8 29
11½	1 8	1 3	0 9	Attenborough	....	....	....	....	8 14	....	9 34	....	....	....	....	....	....	....	....	....	....	6 52	....	....	....	....	....	....	9 18	....	....	8 35
13	1 9	1 4	0 10	Beeston	e	e	....	7 35	8 19	9 14	9 39	10 6	e	e	e	1 33	3 8	f	4 53	e	6 3	6 57	e	e	1045	e	e	....	9 23	e	....	8 40
16½	2 0	1 6	1 0	Nottingham a	1 40	3 48	6 55	7 45	8 30	9 25	9 50	1015	1110	1220	1 10	1 43	3 20	3 50	5 5	5 50	6 15	7 10	7 25	9 5	1055	1 40	3 48	....	9 35	7 15	....	8 50
	FmNotnghm			184, 118 .. d	....	3 56	....	8 0	....	....	....	....	1115	....	....	1 57	....	4 15	....	....	....	....	7 40	....		....	3 56	....	9 45	....	....	
19¼	0 9	0 6	0 3	Carlton & Gedling	....	....	....	8 9	....	....	....	....	1124	....	....	2 4	....	4 23	....	....	....	....	7 49	....		....	....	....	9 52	....	....	
21¼	1 2	0 10	0 5	Burton Joyce	....	....	....	8 15	....	....	....	....	1129	....	....	2 9	....	4 29	....	....	....	....	7 55	....		....	....	....	9 58	....	....	
23¾	1 6	1 2	0 7½	Lowdham	....	....	....	8 21	....	....	....	....	1135	....	....	2 16	....	4 35	....	....	....	....	8 1	....		....	....	....	10 4	....	....	
26	1 10	1 4	0 9½	Thurgarton	....	....	....	8 27	....	....	....	....	1141	....	....	2 22	....	4 40	....	....	....	....	8 7	....		....	....	....	1010	....	....	
27½	2 0	1 6	0 11	Bleasby	....	....	....	8 31	....	....	....	....	1145	....	....	2 27	....	4 45	....	....	....	....	8 11	....		....	....	....	1015	....	....	
29	2 4	1 9	1 0½	Fiskerton	....	4 22	....	8 36	....	....	....	....	1150	....	....	b	....	4 50	....	....	....	....	8 16	....		....	4 22	....	1020	....	....	
29¾	2 6	1 9	1 1	Rolleston Jn. 185	....	....	....	8 39	....	....	....	....	1154	....	....	2 34	....	4 54	....	....	....	....	8 19	....		....	....	....	....	....	....	
32½	3 0	2 3	1 4	Southwell ar	....	....	....	8 48	....	....	....	....	12 5	....	....	2 40	....	5 18	....	....	....	....	8 28	....		....	....	....	....	....	....	
				Southwell dp	....	....	....	7 30	....	....	....	....	1140	....	....	2 20	....	4 19	....	....	....	....	8 5	....		....	....	....	....	....	....	
33½	3 3	2 6	1 5	Newark 109, 106	....	4 33	....	8 51	....	....	....	....	12 4	....	....	2 43	....	5 3	....	....	....	....	8 31	....		....	4 33	....	1029	....	....	
38½	4 3	3 3	1 10	Collingham	....	....	....	9 2	....	....	....	....	1214	....	....	2 53	....	5 13	....	....	....	....	8 42	....		....	....	....	1040	....	....	
41¾	4 6	3 6	2 0½	Swinderby	....	....	....	9 8	....	....	....	....	1220	....	....	2 59	....	5 19	....	....	....	....	8 48	....		....	....	....	1046	....	....	
43½	5 3	3 9	2 3	Thorpe	....	....	....	9 14	....	....	....	....	1226	....	....	3 5	....	5 25	....	....	....	....	8 54	....		....	....	....	1053	....	....	
46	5 4	4 0	2 5½	Hykeham .. [117	....	....	....	9 19	....	....	....	....	b	....	....	b	....	b d	....	....	....	....	8 59	....		....	....	....	1059	....	....	
49½	5 3	4 8	2 8½	Lincoln 221, 116,	....	5 4	....	9 30	....	....	....	....	1238	....	....	3 18	....	5 40	....	....	....	....	9 10	....		....	5 4	....	1110	....	....	
—	15 11	11 6	6 6½	Hull 221 arr	....	7 50	....	1215	....	....	....	....	3 55	....	....	6 0	....	8 40	....	....	....	....	....	....		....	9 10	....	5 30	....	....	

Miles	Frm Lincoln 1 cl. s. d.	2 cl. s. d.	3 cl. s. d.	Corporation Pier,	mrn	mrn	mrn	mrn	mrn (Via Castle Donington.—Extra Fare charged to Derby.)	mrn	mrn	aft	aft	aft (Via Castle Donington.—Extra Fare charged to Derby.)	aft	mrn	aft	aft	aft	aft	aft	mail	aft	aft (Mondays, Fridays, & Saturdays only.)	aft	Sundays. mrn	mrn	aft	aft	aft	mail	aft
				Hull 221 dep	....	....	....	....		....	7 0	....	....		....	9 30	....	....	1240	....	....	5 0	....		....	....	....	....	....	....	4 10	....
				Lincoln ......dep	....	....	7 0	....		....	10 5	....	....		....	1 15	....	....	3 55	....	....	8 10	....		....	....	....	....	5 50	....	8 10	....
3¼	0 8	0 6	0 3	Hykeham	....	....	7 8	....		....	g	....	....		....	h	....	....	4 2	....	....	....	....		....	....	....	....	5 58	....	....	....
5¼	1 2	0 10	0 5½	Thorpe	....	....	7 14	....		....	1015	....	....		....	1 26	....	....	4 8	....	....	....	....		....	....	....	....	6 3	....	....	....
8	1 8	1 2	0 8	Swinderby	....	....	7 20	....		....	1021	....	....		....	h	....	....	4 14	....	....	....	....		....	....	....	....	6 9	....	....	....
10¾	2 0	1 6	0 10½	Collingham	....	....	7 26	....		....	1027	....	....		....	1 35	....	....	4 21	....	....	8 27	....		....	....	....	....	6 14	....	8 27	....
15¾	3 0	2 8	1 3½	Newark 109, 106	....	....	7 39	....		....	1038	....	....		....	1 46	....	....	4 34	....	....	8 37	....		....	....	....	....	6 27	....	8 37	....
22	4 0	3 0	1 10	Southwell ar	....	....	8 48	....		....	1055	....	....		....	2 5	....	....	5 18	....	....	8 55	....		....	....	....	....	....	....	....	....
				Southwell dp	....	....	7 30	....		....	1035	....	....		....	1 45	....	....	4 19	....	....	8 30	....		....	....	....	....	....	....	....	....
19¼	3 8	2 8	1 7½	Rolleston Jn. 185	....	....	7 47	....		....	1045	....	....		....	1 54	....	....	4 43	....	....	8 45	....		....	....	....	....	....	....	....	....
20½	3 9	2 9	1 8	Fiskerton	....	....	7 51	....		....	1049	....	....		....	1 57	....	....	4 47	....	....	8 49	....		....	....	....	....	6 38	....	8 49	....
22	4 0	3 0	1 9½	Bleasby	....	....	7 56	....		....	a	....	....		....	h	....	....	4 52	....	....	....	....		....	....	....	....	6 43	....	....	....
23¾	4 3	3 3	1 11	Thurgarton	....	....	8 1	....		....	1057	....	....		....	2 4	....	....	4 57	....	....	....	....		....	....	....	....	6 48	....	....	....
25½	4 9	3 6	2 1	Lowdham	....	....	8 7	....		....	11 3	....	....		....	2 10	....	....	5 3	....	....	8 59	....		....	....	....	....	6 54	....	8 59	....
27½	5 3	3 9	2 3½	Burton Joyce	....	....	8 12	....		....	1110	....	....		....	2 16	....	....	5 9	....	....	9 5	....		....	....	....	....	7 0	....	9 5	....
29¾	5 6	4 0	2 5½	Carlton & Gedling	....	....	8 18	....		....	1115	....	....		....	2 21	....	....	5 15	....	....	....	....		....	....	....	....	7 5	....	....	....
33	6 3	4 8	2 8½	Nottingham .. a	....	....	8 30	....		....	1125	c	....		....	2 30	....	....	5 25	....	....	9 17	....		....	....	....	....	7 20	....	9 17	....
	FmNotnghm			184, 118 d	7 0	7 45	8c50	9 25	1010	1115	12 0	1225	....	1c5	1c50	2 40	3 15	4 50	5 45	6 40	7 30	9c20	....	10 0	1135	....	9c0	5 40	8c30	....	9c20	1135
36½	0 6	0 4	0 3	Beeston	7 9	7 53	8 59	9 32	1017	1123	12 8	1233	....	1 13	1 58	....	....	4 58	....	6 48	7 38	....	....	1038	1141	....	9 9	....	8 38	....	....	1141
37½	0 9	0 6	0 4½	Attenborough	....	....	9 4	....	....	....	....	....	....	1 18	....	....	....	....	....	....	....	....	....	....	....	....	9 13	....	8 41	....	....	....
39½	1 0	0 8	0 6	Trent 179, 185, a	7 18	8 2	9 9	9 41	1025	1132	1215	1240	....	1 23	2 4	2 52	3 26	5 5	5 58	6 55	7 45	....	....	....	1150	....	9 17	5 52	....	....	....	1150
				190, 178 d	7 30	8 5	9 11	9 50	1031	1143	1225	1243	1253	1 25	2 6	3 4	3 35	5 22	6 10	7 1	7 57	9 35	9 40	....	12 4	9 8	9 20	6 0	8 47	9 17	9 35	12 4
42	1 4	1 0	0 8	Sawley	....	8 11	9 17	....	....	....	1231	....	....	....	2 12	....	3 41	5 29	....	7 7	....	....	9 46	....	....	9 14	9 27	....	8 53	9 23	....	....
42¾	1 6	1 1	0 9	Draycott	....	8 14	9 21	....	....	....	1235	....	....	....	2 15	....	3 45	5 33	....	7 11	....	....	9 50	....	....	9 18	9 30	....	8 57	9 27	....	....
45	1 8	1 2	0 10	Borrowash	7 41	8 20	9 27	....	....	....	1241	....	....	....	2 20	....	3 51	5 40	....	7 17	....	....	9 56	....	....	9 24	9 36	....	9 3	9 32	....	....
46½	1 10	1 4	0 11	Spondon [173, 170	....	8 25	9 32	....	....	....	1246	....	....	....	2 25	....	3 56	5 45	....	7 22	....	....	10 1	....	....	9 28	9 40	....	9 8	9 36	....	....
49½	2 0	1 6	1 0	Derby 186, 185, 181,	7 52	8 34	9 40	1010	11 5	12 5	1255	1 5	1 10	2 5	2 35	3 23	4 5	5 55	6 30	7 30	8 15	9 55	1010	....	1223	9 40	9 55	6 20	9 20	9 48	9 55	1223

a Stops on Saturdays; also daily, when required, to take up for London. **b** Stop to set down from London, on informing the Guard at the preceding stopping Station. c These Trains do not wait for Main Line Trains at Trent. **d** Stops on Wednesdays.

e Stop to set down from Stations North or West of Derby, on informing the Guard at Trent. **f** Stops to set down.

g Stops on Wednesdays; also daily, when required, to take up for London.

h Stops when required to take up for London.

December 1873

NOTTINGHAM, TRENT, and DERBY.—Midland.

Week Days.

Fares 1 cl. s. d.	3 cl. s. d.		mrn	mrn (Except Mondays.)	mrn (Mons. only.)	mrn (Mondays only.)	mrn (Except Mondays.)	3 cl.	mrn	mrn	mrn	mrn	mrn (Except Saturdays.)	mrn	mrn	mrn	mrn	mrn	mrn	mrn	mrn	mrn	mrn
		Nottingham ......dep.	1245	2 42	....	4 35	4 45	....	5 55	6 5	6 25	6 32	6 47	7 25	7 35	7 47	8 0	8 20	8 34	8 43	9 5	9 15	....
0 6	0 3	Beeston	....	a	....	4 42	4 52	....	6 2	6 11	6 32	6 39	b	7 31	7 44	7 55	8 7	8 26	8 41	....	n	9 21	....
0 8	0 4½	Attenborough	....		....	....	....	....	....	....	....	....		7 35	....	7 59	8 11	....	....	....	....	....	....
0 10	0 6	Trent 467, 458 arr.	1255	j	....	4 49	4 58	....	6 8	....	6 38	6 46		7 41	7 50	8 3	8 16	....	8 47	8 53	9 15	....	....
		dep.	....		3 5			....	....	....	6 40	....		7 45	....	8 5	....	k	....	8 55	9 18	....	9 33
1 1	0 7	Sawley Junction	....					....	....	....	....	....		....	....	8 9	....	....	....	....	....	....	9 37
1 2	0 8	Sawley	....					....	....	....	....	....		....	....	8 13	....	....	....	....	....	....	....
1 4	0 9	Draycott ....[brook	....					5 22	....	....	6 47	....		....	....	8 16	....	....	....	9 1	....	....	9 41
1 6	0 10	Borrowash, for Ock-	....					5 28	....	....	6 53	....		....	....	8 22	....	....	....	9 7	....	....	9 47
1 8	0 11	Spondon	....					5 33	....	....	6 57	....		....	....	8 27	....	....	....	9 11	....	....	9 51
1 9	1 0	Derby 494, 476..arr.	....	3 10	3 20			5 45	....	....	7 4	....		8 0	....	8 34	....	....	....	9 20	9 32	....	9 57

Week Days—*Continued.*

	mrn	mrn	mrn	mrn	mrn	mrn	mrn	aft	aft	aft	aft	aft (Sats. only.)	aft	aft	aft	aft	aft	aft	aft (Weds. only.)	aft	aft	aft	aft
Nottingham ......dep.	9 42	9 55	1050	1112	1123	....	1145	1222	1232	1256	1 0		1 26	1 30	1 50	2 5	2 22	2 25	3 3	3 5	3 25	3 32	3 50
Beeston	9 48	....	1057	1118	b	....	1151	d	1239	....	1 7		1 33	1 37	1 56	2 12	2 28	2 32	i	3 12	....	3 39	3 57
Attenborough	....	....	11 1	....	....	....	1155	....	....	1 6	1 12		....	1 41	....	....	....	Sat.	....	....	....	3 43	....
Trent 469, 458 arr.	9 55	10 6	11 4	1125	1133	....	12 0	1234	1246	....	1 16		1 39	....	2 3	2 13	2 35	2 38	3 15	3 18	3 35	3 47	4 3
dep.	10 5	....	....	1128		1139	12 2	1237	....	....		1 23	1 41	....	....	2 21	2 38	....		3 20	3 39	3 49	....
Sawley Junction	....	....	....	....	....	1143	....	....	....	....	....	1 26	....	....	....	2 25	....	....		....	....	3 53	....
Sawley	....	....	....	....	....	1147	....	....	....	....	....	1 30	....	....	....	....	....	....		....	....	3 57	....
Draycott ....[brook	....	....	....	....	....	1150	c	....	....	....	....	1 33	....	....	....	2 29	....	....		e	....	4 0	....
Borrowash, for Ock-	....	....	....	....	....	1156	....	....	....	....	....	1 39	....	....	....	2 35	....	....		....	....	4 6	....
Spondon	....	....	....	....	....	12 0	....	....	....	....	....	1 43	....	....	....	2 39	....	....		....	....	4 10	....
Derby 494, 476..arr.	1018	....	....	1141	....	1210	1218	1250	....	....	....	1 51	1 55	....	....	2 46	2 51	....		3 33	3 52	4 20	....

Week Days—*Continued.*

	aft	aft	aft	aft	aft	aft	aft	aft	aft	aft	aft	aft	aft	aft	aft	aft	aft	aft	aft	aft	aft	aft	aft
Nottingham ......dep.	4 0	4 7	4 25	4 40	5 6	5 15	5 25	6 0	6 10	6 48	6 58	7 15	7 30	7 38	7 57	8 26	....	....	9 19	9 30	1035	1040	....
Beeston	....	....	....	4 49	5 13	....	5 31	6 6	6 16	6 56	7 5	f	7 37	b	8 4	8 32	....	....	....	9 36	1042	1047	....
Attenborough	....	....	....	4 54	....	....	5 35	....	....	7 0	....	....	7 41	....	....	8 35	....	....	....	9 40	1046	....	....
Trent 469, 460 arr.	....	4 17	4 35	5 0	5 19	5 25	5 40	....	6 23	7 5	7 11	7 27	7 45	7 48	8 10	8 41	....	....	9 29	9 45	1050	1053	....
dep.	m	4 19	....	....	5 22	5 40	....	....	6 26	7 8	....	7 29	....	....	....	8 44	8 48	9 18	9 32	....	1052	....	1114
Sawley Junction	....	....	....	....	....	5 44	....	....	....	7 11	....	....	....	....	....	....	8 52	....	....	....	....	....	Sat.
Sawley	....	....	....	....	....	....	....	....	....	7 15	....	....	....	....	....	....	....	....	....	....	....	....	....
Draycott ....[brook	....	....	....	....	....	5 48	....	....	....	7 18	....	l	....	....	....	....	8 56	....	....	....	....	....	1121
Borrowash, for Ock-	....	....	....	....	....	5 54	....	....	....	7 24	....	g	....	....	....	8 52	9 2	....	....	....	....	....	1127
Spondon	....	....	....	....	....	5 58	....	....	....	7 29	....	....	....	....	....	....	9 8	....	....	....	....	....	1132
Derby 496, 477..arr.	....	4 32	....	....	5 35	6 7	....	....	6 39	7 38	....	7 48	....	....	....	9 4	9 14	9 31	9 47	....	11 5	....	1142

	Week Days—*Continued.* aft (Except Saturdays.)	aft (Saturdays only.)	aft (Saturdays only.)	aft	Sundays. mrn	mrn	mrn	mrn	mrn	mrn	mrn	mrn	mrn	aft	aft	aft	aft	aft	aft	aft	aft	aft	aft
Nottingham ......dep.	1055	11 0	1115	1130	....	1235	1245	2 42	6 25	7 25	8 10	9 0	9 35	1 30	1 55	5 17	5 45	6 40	....	8 25	8 45	9 19	1140
Beeston	11 3	11 9	1124	1136	....	....	....	....	6 32	7 32	8 17	9 8	9 42	1 37	2 2	5 24	5 52	h	....	8 32	8 51	....	1148
Attenborough	11 7		1129	....	....	....	....	....	....	....	....	9 12	....	....	....	....	5 57	....	....	....	8 55	....	....
Trent 473, 464 arr.				1143	....	1245	1255	j	....	7 39	8 23	9 17	9 48	1 43	2 10	5 30	6 2	6 53	....	8 40	9 0	9 29	1157
dep.				1146	1212	1247	....	....	....	....	....	9 20	....	1 51	2 21	5 32	....	6 56	7 8	....	9 7	9 32	1158
Sawley Junction				....	....	....	....	....	....	....	....	9 25	....	....	....	....	....	....	....	....	9 11	....	....
Sawley				....	....	....	....	....	....	....	....	....	....	....	....	....	....	....	....	....	....	....	....
Draycott ....[brook				....	....	....	....	....	....	....	....	9 31	....	....	....	5 39	....	....	....	....	9 15	....	....
Borrowash, for Ock-				....	....	....	....	....	....	....	....	9 37	....	....	....	5 45	....	....	....	....	9 21	....	....
Spondon				....	....	....	....	....	....	....	....	9 41	....	....	....	5 49	....	....	....	....	9 25	....	....
Derby 496, 478..arr.				1159	1225	1 0	....	3 10	....	....	....	9 50	....	2 5	2 34	5 56	....	7 10	7 23	....	9 32	9 47	1215

a Stops when required to take up for Manchester and Liverpool. **b** Stop when required to take up for London. **c** Stops when required to set down, or to take up for Manchester. **d** Stops when required to take up for North or West of Derby. **e** Stops when required to take up for Sheffield and beyond. **f** Stops when required to take up for beyond Marple. **g** Stops when required to set down from the Peterboro', Lincoln, Mansfield and Erewash Valley Lines. **h** Stops when required to take up for Birmingham and beyond; also for South of Leicester. **i** Stops when required to take up for Loughboro' and beyond. **j** Stop when required to set down. **k** Stops when required to take up for Birmingham and beyond. **l** Stops when required to set down from the Erewash Valley Line. **m** Stops on Thursdays when required to take up from Loughboro' for Burton and beyond. **n** Stops on Mondays and Thursdays when required to take up for Burton and beyond.

January 1901

NOTTINGHAM, TRENT, and DERBY.—Midland.

Week Days.

Miles		mrn (Except Mondays.)	mrn	mrn	mrn	mrn	mrn	mrn	mrn	mrn	mrn	mrn	mrn	mrn	mrn	mrn	mrn	mrn	mrn	mrn	mrn	mrn	mrn
	Nottingham ....dep.	1230	1 40	4 30	5 35	5 50	6 5	6 12	6 43	....	7 0	7 10	7 33	7 40	7 50	8 15	8 23	....	9 5	9 12	9 40	9 50	10 0
3¾	Beeston	....	1 48	4 38	5 43	5 58	6 13	6 20	6 51	....	7 8	7 18	7 41	7 50	7 58	8 23	8 31	....	....	9 20	9 48	9 58	....
4¾	Attenborough	....	....	....	5 47	6 3	6 17	6 24	....	....	....	7 22	7 45	....	8 2	8 27	....	....	....	9 24	9 52	....	....
6¾	**Trent** 502, 513... arr.	1241	1 54	4 44	....	6 8	6 22	6 29	....	....	7 14	7 27	7 50	....	....	8 32	8 37	....	9 16	....	9 57	10 4	....
	dep.		....	....	....	....	6 25	....	....	7 4	7 22	....	7 58	....	....	8 35	....	9 1	9 20	....	....	1014	....
7¾	Sawley Junction		....	....	....	....	....	....	....	7 9	....	....	8 4	....	....	....	....	9 5	....	....	....	1019	....
9	Sawley		....	....	....	....	....	....	....	....	....	....	8 8	....	....	....	....	....	....	....	....	....	....
9¾	Draycott		....	....	....	....	6 34	....	....	7 15	....	....	8 12	....	....	....	....	....	....	....	....	1024	....
12	Borrowash*		....	....	....	....	6 41	....	....	7 22	....	....	8 19	....	....	....	....	9 13	....	....	....	1031	....
13¾	Spondon .... [530		....	....	....	....	6 47	....	....	7 26	7 35	....	8 26	....	....	....	....	9 18	....	....	....	1036	....
16	**Derby** ‖ 410, 522, arr.		....	....	....	....	6 58	....	....	7 35	7 43	....	8 35	8 10	....	8 50	....	9 29	9 35	....	....	1044	1025

Week Days—*Continued.*

	mrn	mrn	mrn	mrn	mrn	aft	aft	aft	aft	aft (Sats. only.)	aft	aft	aft	aft	aft	aft	aft	aft	aft	aft	aft	aft	aft
Nottingham ....dep.	10 8	1045	11 1	1118	1122	12 0	1228	1245	1 2	1 10	1 25	1 44	1 55	2 3	2 25	2 30	2 40	3 30	3 55	4 4	4 45	5 5	5 13
Beeston	....	1053	....	1126	1130	12 8	1236	1253	1 10	1 19	....	1 52	2 4	2 11	....	2 40	2 48	3 38	4 3	4 12	4 53	5 14	5 21
Attenborough	....	1057	....	....	1134	....	....	1258	1 14	1 22	....	....	....	2 15	....	....	....	....	4 7	....	....	....	5 25
Trent 502, 513... arr.	1019	11 2	....	1132	....	1214	1242	....	1 19	1 28	1 36	....	2 10	2 20	2 36	....	....	3 44	4 12	....	5 0	5 20	5 30
dep.	....	....	....	1137	....	1218	....	....	1 25		....	....	2 13	2 23	....	....	....	3 47	4 15	....	5 2	....	5 38
Sawley Junction	....	....	....	1143	....	....	....	....	1 30		....	....	....	2 28	....	....	....	....	4 20	....	....	....	5 44
Sawley	....	....	....	1147	....	....	....	....	1 34		....	....	....	....	....	....	....	....	4 24	....	....	....	5 48
Draycott	....	....	....	1151	....	....	....	....	1 38		....	....	....	2 33	....	....	....	....	4 28	....	....	....	5 52
Borrowash*	....	....	....	1157	....	....	....	....	1 44		....	....	....	2 40	....	....	....	....	4 34	....	....	....	5 58
Spondon .... [530	....	....	....	12 2	....	....	....	....	1 49		....	....	....	2 45	....	....	....	....	4 40	....	....	....	6 3
Derby ‖ 410, 522, arr.	....	....	1126	1211	....	1235	....	....	1 58		....	....	2 30	2 53	....	3 3	....	4 2	4 50	....	5 18	....	6 14

Week Days—*Continued.*

	aft	aft	aft		aft	aft	aft	aft	aft	aft (Sats. only.)	aft	aft	aft (Sats. only.)	aft	aft (Sats. only.)	aft (Sats. only.)	aft (Except Saturdays.)	aft (Sats. only.)	aft			
Nottingham ....dep.	5 38	6 3	6 13	....	6 50	7 17	7 45	8 20	8 30	9 0	9 11	9 25	9 35	9 45	1030	1040	1042	11 0	1150	....	....	....
Beeston	5 46	6 11	6 21	....	6 58	7 25	7 53	8 28	8 38	9 8	....	9 33	9 43	9 53	1038	1048	1050	11 8	1159	....	....	....
Attenborough	....	6 16	....	....	....	7 29	7 57	....	....	9 12	....	9 38	9 47	9 57	1043	1052	1055	1112	....	....	....	....
Trent 502, 513... arr.	5 52	....	6 27	....	7 4	7 35	8 2	8 34	8 44		9 22	9 44	9 52	10 2		1057			12 5	....	....	....
dep.	....	....	6 32	....	7 10	....	8 6	8 38	....		9 25	9 47		....		11 0			12 8	....	....	....
Sawley Junction	....	....	....	....	....	....	8 11	....	....		....	9 53		....		11 5			....	....	....	....
Sawley	....	....	....	....	....	....		....	....		....	....		....		....			....	....	....	....
Draycott	....	....	....	....	....	....	8 16	....	....		....	9 58		....		1110			....	....	....	....
Borrowash*	....	....	....	....	....	....	8 22	....	....		....	10 4		....		1116			....	....	....	....
Spondon .... [530	....	....	....	....	....	....	8 27	....	....		....	10 8		....		1121			....	....	....	....
Derby ‖ 410, 522, arr.	....	....	6 47	....	7 26	....	8 35	8 55	....		9 43	1017		....		1130			1225	....	....	....

Sundays.

	mrn	mrn	mrn	mrn	mrn	mrn	mrn	aft	aft	aft	aft	aft	aft	aft	aft	aft	
Nottingham ....dep.	1230	1 40	5 55	7 10	....	8 5	9 30	1 15	2 0	5 0	5 20	6 45	8 42	9 11	9 20	1150	....
Beeston	....	1 48	6 3	7 18	....	8 14	9 38	1 23	2 8	5 8	....	6 53	8 50	....	9 28	1159	....
Attenborough	....	....	6 8	7 22	....	....	9 43	....	....	5 12	....	....	8 54	....	9 32	....	....
Trent 508, 519.. arr.	1241	1 54	....	7 27	....	8 20	9 48	1 29	2 14	5 17	5 31	6 59	9 0	9 22	9 37	12 5	....
dep.	....	....	....	....	8 15	....	9 58	1 35	2 18	5 20	5 44	7 4	....	9 25	9 39	12 8	....
Sawley Junction	....	....	....	....	....	....	10 3	....	....	....	....	....	....	....	9 44	....	....
Sawley	....	....	....	....	....	....	....	....	....	....	....	....	....	....	....	....	....
Draycott	....	....	....	....	8 24	....	10 8	....	2 25	5 28	....	....	....	....	9 50	....	....
Barrowash	....	....	....	....	8 31	....	1014	....	2 31	5 35	....	....	....	....	9 55	....	....
Spondon	....	....	....	....	8 36	....	1018	....	2 36	5 42	....	....	....	....	10 1	....	....
Derby ‖ 524, 532..arr.	....	....	....	....	8 45	....	1026	1 50	2 46	5 50	6 0	7 22	....	9 43	1010	1225	....

* Station for Ockbrook (1¼ miles).
‖ Over 1 mile to Great Northern (Friargate) Station.

July 1921

March 1951

NOTTINGHAM, TRENT, and DERBY

Week Days (a.m. ... p.m)

Miles	HOURS	D 3		5		6		6		6	7	7		7		7	8	8		9	9
	Nottingham (City).... dep	.	.	56	.	0	.	24	.	43	0	16	.	41	.	53	0	15	.	0	25
3¾	Beeston	.	.	**6**	.	Y14	.	34	.	53	10	26	.	51	.	**2**	9	25	.	10	.
4¾	Attenborough	.	.	.	.	18	.	38	.	.	14	30	.	.	.	6	14	29	.	.	.
6¾	Trent .... arr	.	.	12	.	.	.	44	.	59	19	35	.	.	.	11	.	34	.	16	36
	dep	7	.	.	.	.	.	48	.	.	22	.	.	.	.	12	.	36	.	19	.
7¾	Sawley Junction **A**	.	.	.	.	.	.	53	.	.	27	.	.	**1**	.	16	.	.	.	.	.
9¾	Draycott **B**	.	.	.	.	.	.	58	.	.	.	.	.	.	.	21	.	.	.	.	.
12¼	Borrowash **C**	.	.	.	.	.	.	**4**	.	.	.	.	.	.	.	26	.	.	.	29	.
13¾	Spondon	.	.	.	.	.	.	Y12	.	.	36	.	.	.	.	31	.	47	.	.	.
16	Derby (Midland) ...... arr	28	.	.	.	.	.	21	.	.	42	.	.	17	.	37	.	53	.	36	.

Miles	HOURS		10	10		11	S 12		11		12	S 12		S 12	12		S 1	1		2	2		3		4	E 5	E 5		5	5		5		6
	Nottingham (City).... dep	.	30	45	.	10	.	.	55	.	3	15	.	24	40	.	8	25	.	5	16	.	40	.	12	0	.	.	8	15	.	43	.	4
3¾	Beeston	.	.	55	.	20	.	.	**5**	.	13	25	.	34	50	.	18	35	.	15	25	.	50	.	.	10	.	.	18	25	.	53	.	14
4¾	Attenborough	.	.	59	.	24	.	.	9	.	17	29	.	38	54	.	22	.	.	19	29	.	54	.	.	14	.	.	.	29	.	59	.	18
6¾	Trent .... arr	.	41	**4**	.	29	.	.	.	.	22	34	.	.	59	.	27	41	.	24	.	.	59	.	25	.	.	.	24	34	.	.	.	23
	dep	.	43	.	.	31	.	.	.	.	26	.	.	.	.	.	29	.	.	26	.	.	.	.	27	.	.	.	.	36	.	.	.	.
7¾	Sawley Junction **A**	.	.	.	.	36	.	.	.	.	31	.	.	.	.	.	34	.	.	31	.	.	.	.	.	.	.	.	.	41	.	.	.	.
9¾	Draycott **B**	.	.	.	.	41	.	.	.	.	.	.	.	.	.	.	39	.	.	.	.	.	.	.	.	.	.	.	.	46	.	.	.	.
12¼	Borrowash **C**	.	.	.	.	47	.	.	.	.	.	.	.	.	.	.	45	.	.	.	.	.	.	.	.	.	.	.	.	52	.	.	.	.
13¾	Spondon	.	.	.	.	52	8	.	.	.	.	.	.	.	.	.	50	.	.	.	.	.	.	.	.	.	37	.	.	57	.	.	.	.
16	Derby (Midland) ...... arr	.	58	.	.	59	15	.	.	.	43	.	.	.	.	.	57	.	.	44	.	.	.	.	42	.	45	.	.	**6**	.	.	.	.

Week Days—*continued* (p.m. ... p.m.)

HOURS	6		6	7	7		7	8	9		S 9	9			10	10		11		
Nottingham (City).... dep	9	.	58	10	45	.	59	20	6	.	25	30	.	.	23	50	.	55	.	.
Beeston	19	.	**8**	20	55	.	**9**	30	.	.	35	40	.	.	33	**0**	.	**5**	.	.
Attenborough	24	.	12	24	59	.	13	.	.	.	39	44	.	.	37	4	.	.	.	.
Trent .... arr	29	.	17	29	.	.	18	36	17	.	44	.	.	.	42	9	.	11	.	.
dep	30	.	.	31	.	.	.	38	19	.	46	.	.	.	.	11	.	13	.	.
Sawley Junction **A**	35	.	.	36	.	.	.	43	.	.	51	.	.	.	.	16	.	18	.	.
Draycott **B**	.	.	.	41	.	.	.	.	.	.	56	.	.	.	.	.	.	.	.	.
Borrowash **C**	.	.	.	47	.	.	.	.	.	.	**2**	.	.	.	.	.	.	.	.	.
Spondon	45	.	.	52	.	.	.	52	.	.	7	.	.	.	.	.	.	.	.	.
Derby (Midland) ...... arr	55	.	.	59	.	.	.	58	37	.	14	.	.	.	.	31	.	31	.	.

Sundays (a.m. ... p.m.)

HOURS	3		6	6		7		7		9		11	12		1		2		3	4	4	5		5	5		6		9	9	9	10	11	11		
Nottingham (City).... dep	.	.	7	40	.	23	.	48	.	35	.	58	25	.	38	.	0	.	40	.	25	8	.	18	35	.	45	.	6	15	40	.	14	55	.	.
Beeston	.	.	16	50	.	33	.	58	.	45	.	**8**	35	.	48	.	10	.	50	.	35	18	.	.	45	.	55	.	.	25	50	.	24	**5**	.	.
Attenborough	.	.	.	.	.	.	.	.	.	49	.	12	.	.	52	.	14	.	.	.	39	.	.	.	.	.	.	.	.	29	54	.	28	.	.	.
Trent .... arr	.	.	.	56	.	39	.	**4**	.	54	.	17	41	.	57	.	19	.	57	.	44	24	.	31	51	.	**1**	.	17	34	59	.	33	11	.	.
dep	23	.	.	57	.	.	.	.	.	56	.	.	**0**	.	.	.	21	.	.	13	46	.	.	.	53	.	3	.	19	.	**1**	58	35	13	.	.
Sawley Junction **A**	.	.	.	**2**	.	.	.	.	.	**1**	.	.	.	.	.	.	26	.	.	.	51	.	.	.	.	.	.	.	.	.	6	.	.	18	.	.
Draycott **B**	.	.	.	.	.	.	.	.	.	.	.	.	.	.	.	.	.	.	.	.	.	.	.	.	.	.	.	.	.	.	.	.	.	.	.	.
Borrowash **C**	.	.	.	.	.	.	.	.	.	.	.	.	.	.	.	.	.	.	.	.	.	.	.	.	.	.	.	.	.	.	.	.	.	.	.	.
Spondon	.	.	.	11	.	.	.	.	.	10	.	.	.	.	.	.	.	.	.	.	**0**	.	.	.	.	.	.	.	.	.	15	.	.	.	.	.
Derby (Midland) ...... arr	44	.	.	17	.	.	.	.	.	16	.	.	15	.	.	.	38	.	.	30	7	.	.	.	**8**	.	18	.	37	.	21	**20**	50	31	.	.

A Sawley Junction for Long Eaton
B Draycott and Breaston
C Station for Ockbrook (1¼ miles)
D Mondays only
E Except Saturdays
F Except Mondays
L Commences 25th March. Also on Good Friday 23rd March
S Saturdays only
X Through Carriages to St. Pancras
Y Arr. 5 minutes *earlier*
W Train temporarily withdrawn

Where the MINUTES under the Hours change to a LOWER figure and DARKER type it indicates the NEXT HOUR

NOTTINGHAM

II. We begin our journey at the centre station on the right page of this 1923 map and continue to the lower left corner of the left one. Other destinations can be found on map I. The GCR was built from top to bottom of the right page.

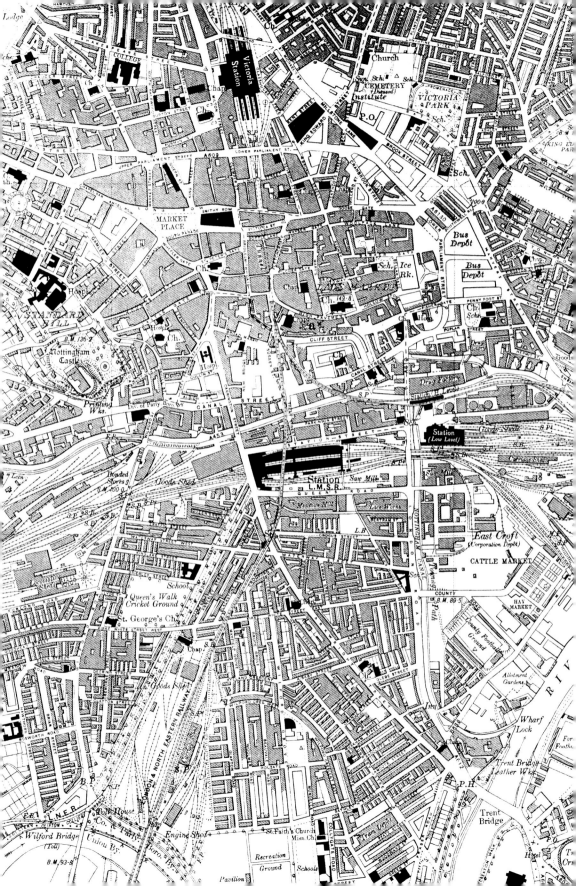

1.   This view northwest of the first station (a terminus) is from near the site of Queens Road and has Nottingham Castle in the background. The frontages of both the first and second stations appear in our album, *Kettering to Nottingham* (nos 105 & 106). The highway over the bridge was named Flood Road on the 1853 map. By the 1880s, there were 170 men employed at the station. By 1890, there were still only three platforms. (F.S.Williams)

2.   This is the frontage of the third station, soon after it was officially opened on 17th January 1904. The style was termed Edwardian Baroque Revival. There is evidence of the tramway, which was in use from 1901 to 1936. The diagonal at the front of the tram is part of the staircase to its open top seats. Glass doors were fitted to the station in 2014. (J.Suter coll.)

3.   It is March 1933 and sunlit is 0-4-4T no. 1327, designated 1P. This type was introduced in 1881 and just one was allocated to Derby engine shed, which is illustrated in pictures 109 onwards. (W.Taylor coll.)

4.   There was serious flooding in 1875 and again in 1947. As snows melted, the River Trent burst its banks at Wilford and West Bridgford. The flood waters reached as far as here and gained a record height on 19th March. No. 2557 was a 1936 2-6-4T. The suffix CITY was used from 25th September 1950 to 18th June 1951. Above is the former GCR bowstring girder bridge. This became redundant in 1973 and was finally dismantled in the early 1980s. The alignment was later used for a new tramway bridge and station. (R.Humm coll.)

5. Waiting to leave from platform 7 on 24th July 2001 is Central Trains no. 158785, bound for Birmingham New Street. The station was extensively renovated in 2013. It had the suffix MIDLAND from 18th June 1951 to 6th May 1970. Trams now run over the bridge behind the camera. On 12th January 2018, the newly renovated buildings were badly damaged by fire. It had started in the women's toilet in the newly-built section. (P.Jones)

III. The layout and shed details are seen in 2013. (©TRACKmaps)

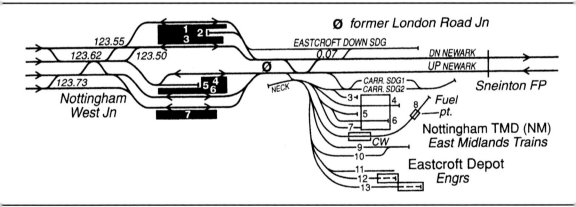

For pictures of trolleybuses in Nottingham, please see our *Nottinghamshire and Derbyshire Trolleybuses*. **There is also an album called** *Nottinghamshire and Derbyshire Tramway.*

For views of all the city's stations, please see the following albums: *Leicester to Nottingham, Kettering to Nottingham, Nottingham to Lincoln, Nottingham to Boston, Loughborough to Nottingham, Nottingham towards Kirkby in Ashfield (the GCR Route 1898 to 1966)* **and** *Nottingham to Mansfield.*

WEST OF NOTTINGHAM

6.   No. 45119 is seen departing with a St Pancras to Sheffield service on 16th September 1982. The massive goods shed had been closed on 3rd January 1966. (T.Heavyside)

IV. The MR diagram of 1912 has its station on the right, with the GCR passing over it.

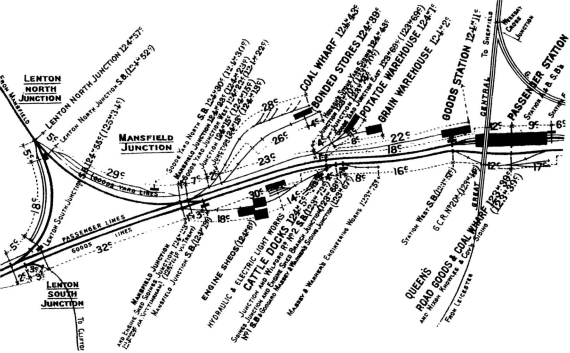

7.   A view west on 13th May 2000 features no. 60037 hauling empty tanks bound for one of the refineries at Immingham. The disused three bridge spans were earlier over the tracks to the main goods yard. Beyond them is the new Income Tax Office, while the gates on the right give security to the Magistrates Office. (R.J.Stewart-Smith)

8.   A four-car Meridian unit leaves westwards on 2nd July 2005, forming the 12.52 departure to London St Pancras. As with so many urban locations, the land on both sides of the line was once occupied by sidings and goods facilities, now replaced by car parks and non-railway development. The station's impressive clock tower appears again. (P.D.Shannon)

Engine sheds

9.   The sheds are below centre of map II, just to the right of the join. The code was 16A in 1948-63 and 16D until closure to steam in 1965. They housed 144 locos in 1950 and 96 in 1959. Total closure was in November 1967. Nottingham Castle is on the hill. Near us is LMS 8F 2-8-0 no. 8071. It was lost during military service in World War II. The photo is from July 1938. (W.Taylor coll.)

10.   We are at the west end on 28th April 1957, with all three engine sheds and the water tank in the background. These sheds all had central turntables. The nearest building is the coaling shed. On the left is the breakdown crane. (W.Taylor coll.)

Mansfield Junction

11.   Goods Yard North Box is on the right and is shown on map IV. We are looking west with the fogman's hut and stove on the left. He would apply detonators to the rail head, when the driver was unable to see the signals. The 1902 box had a 65-lever frame. The structure had been enlarged in 1933 and closed on 7th December 1969. (J.Alsop coll.)

Lenton South Junction

12.   The signal box is behind the train in this view east in April 1956. It had a 53-lever frame and was in use until 17th May 1981. No. 40931 was an ex-LMS 4P and is destined for Bakewell. (W.Taylor coll.)

13. We see the same box again, but on 2nd July 1963. Signalled westwards is no. 45238, a well-coaled 4-6-0 bound for its next duty. The lines under the footbridge (right) served Clifton Colliery. It was worked from 1867 to 1968. (A.F.Bullimore)

Hotel advertisements from *Bradshaw*, July 1910.

EAST OF BEESTON

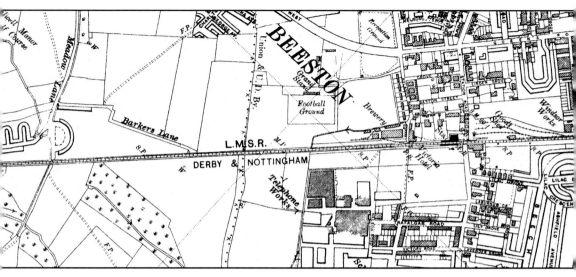

Va. Beeston station, goods yard and brewery siding are on the left page, while the other extensive sidings are east of Humber Road South. This 1939 edition is scaled at about 8ins to 1 mile.

Vb. This diagram indicates the arrangement in 2005. (©TRACKmaps)

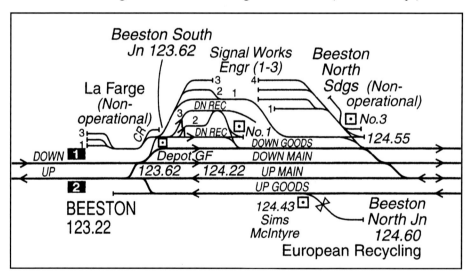

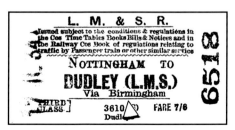

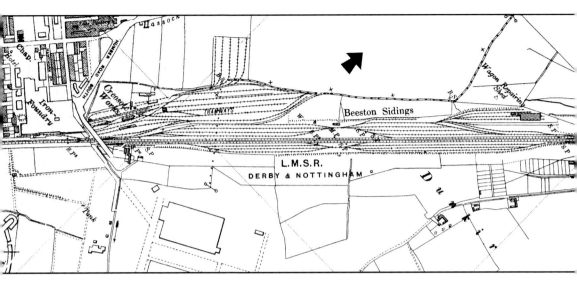

Beeston Creosote Works

14. The works had its own 3ft gauge tram system and a boundary fence can be found with a lens, on the map above. It is beyond the two tracks, below the word TRAMWAYS. It was originally worked by a Motor Rail Simplex petrol loco supplied new in 1919, but this was replaced in 1945 by *Batley*, a 1924 Bagnall 0-4-0ST that had formerly worked on various reservoir contracts. It is seen below. (A.Neale coll.)

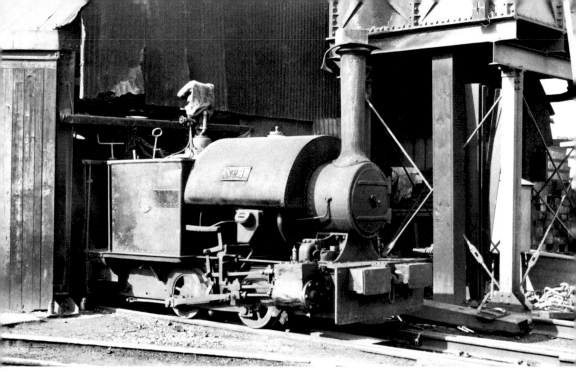

15. After *Batley* was withdrawn and scrapped in October 1955, it was replaced by *No. 1*, a smaller 1911 Bagnall 0-4-0ST from a granite quarry at Nuneaton. The works had been built by the MR in 1880 and gradually closed down in the mid-1960s. (F.Jones)

16. Creosoted sleepers are stacked on the left, having been treated under pressure in autoclaves in the largest building. The prominent building with the bell tower in the left background is Nottingham University. (Colour-Rail.com)

→ 17. Beeston Freightliner Terminal had an active life of just under 18 years before falling victim to the Freightliner cutbacks of April 1987. In later years, wagons were tripped from Beeston to Birmingham Lawley Street to connect with trunk Freightliner trains. No. 31167 departs with the 15.23 trip to Lawley Street on 27th July 1984. (P.D.Shannon)

18. No. 47292 runs east with discharged fuel tanks from Langley to Lindsey Refinery on the same day. In the background lies the Blue Circle cement terminal, with a class 08 shunter present. (P.D.Shannon)

19. Unit 170502 passes the site of Beeston Freightliner terminal on 2nd July 2005, forming the 13.36 from Nottingham to Hereford. The Freightliner site would later be used as a railway infrastructure depot, specialising in points and crossings. (P.D.Shannon)

BEESTON

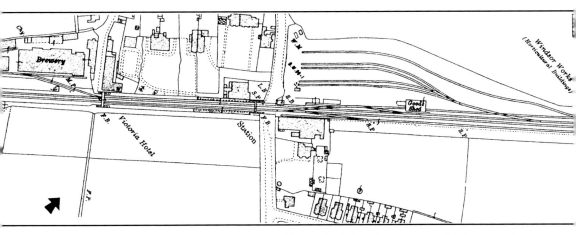

VI. The 1914 edition is seen at about 15ins to 1 mile. On the left is the brewery, which was for long owned by J. Shipstone & Sons Ltd. See captions 29 and 30 for details.

20.   We start with two postcards from around 1900. The nearest bridge could be used by residents unwilling to wait for slow moving through trains. The distant one was probably the first, as it was close to the hotel. (J.Alsop coll.)

21.   The proximity of the goods shed and the cattle dock is evident here. The station was used by many commuters from an early date, although that name did not arrive from the USA until the 1950s. (J.Alsop coll.)

22.   This view from the footbridge on 5th September 1953 includes the cattle dock, which is accommodating a horse box. They were provided with a compartment for an attendant for whom a concessionary fare was available. Running in is 4P 4-4-0 no. 41070, bound for Derby. In the left background is the 5-ton crane. An advertisement in the foreground is 'Introducing Heinz Ideal Sauce', which was described as a rich, thick, brown sauce. (J.Suter coll.)

23. The signal box had 25 levers and a gate wheel. Built in 1891, it lasted until 7th December 1969. A bridge replaced the level crossing in 1969. The DMU is working the 12.20 Nottingham to Sheffield on 12th February 1960. The end styling became known as 'Cats' Whiskers' very widely. It was short lived. (R.Humm coll.)

↓ 24. The Victoria Hotel is nearest and beyond it is part of the brewery. It is 8th June 1962 and class 8F 2-8-0 no. 48749 is hauling an extremely lengthy rake of empty coal wagons. On the left is a ¼ mile post. (Milepost 92½)

25. The goods shed and yard closed on 29th November 1969. This and the next picture are from 16th August 1967. The facilities seem already to have become little used. (R.J.Essery/R.S.Carpenter coll.)

26. The original cottage-style building was replaced in 1847 with this larger structure, with some fine architectural features, notably ornate barge boards. (R.J.Essery/R.S.Carpenter coll.)

27. The platform canopies were extended west with the wooden and steel parts seen. They came from Southwell station. Sprinter no. 150150 is working the 11.32 Nottingham to Leeds service on 7th February 1987. (A.C.Hartless)

28. The station became a listed structure in 1987. Passengers numbered over 0.5 million at the station in 2014. The unit number is 170117. The original 1871 canopy section is glazed, with wrought iron brackets. Between 20th July and 25th August 2013, the services from the station were reduced because of the Nottingham remodelling and resignalling scheme. It acted as a terminus for trains from London via East Midlands Parkway and from Derby, with a frequent rail-replacement shuttle bus running to and from Nottingham, while the western end of the station and approach lines were improved. The Nottingham Express Transit tram service started in Beeston Centre on 25th August 2015. (Colour-Rail.com)

29. Mixed freight is being hauled by an outside framed MR 2-4-0. Victoria Hotel can be glimpsed beside its smokebox. (R.Humm coll.)

30. Passing in April 1969 is a class 45 diesel. In 2013, Beeston lost not only part of its heritage but also an historical industrial site, that of The Beeston Brewery Company. The brewery and maltings were founded in the late 1870s; the brewery operations were carried out in the southwest end of the site, whilst the maltings occupied the northeast end. In 1922, Shipstone and Sons Ltd took over the factory and brewing ceased on the site. The entire building was then converted to a maltings in 1924. The company was the first in England to have pneumatic maltings, where air is forced through the batches of growing grain. With malt being produced at Beeston since 1878, the closure saw the demise of Nottingham's once extensive flour malting industry. (B.Gant/Colour-Rail.com)

ATTENBOROUGH

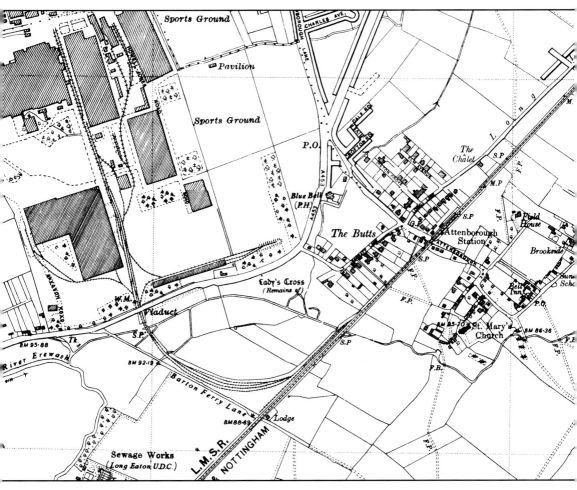

VII. The 1939 edition at 6ins to 1 mile reveals that there was no goods yard. The extensive sidings, top left, served the Army and are described in caption 41.

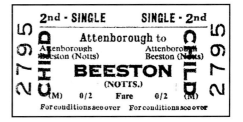

31.   Spelt without 'UGH', the box is seen in MR days, with the wicket gate half-obscured. This was for use by pedestrians, under the control of one of the signalman's levers. There were 22 levers in total and they were in use from 1894 to 27th June 1982, but only for level crossing control from 7th December 1969. (R.Humm coll.)

32.   Initially, there was a halt here from 1st December 1856 until 1st November 1858 and it had the suffix 'Gate'. The station was opened on 1st September 1864; the footbridge followed later. The station was renamed Chilwell for five months in 1937, evidently an unpopular move. (J.Alsop coll.)

33.   In the early years, before the buildings arrived, the gate keeper issued tickets to passengers. The buildings seen in this undated view were erected in 1864. (R.Humm coll.)

34.   The panorama from the footbridge on 7th January 1957 includes a light engine with its drain cocks open and 2-6-4T no. 42336 with one passenger evident. The platforms had been greatly lengthened for Army traffic. (R.Humm coll.)

35. Floor cleaning was in progress on the day that an LCGB Special Train ran through behind 4-6-2 no. 70052 *Firth of Tay* on 24th April 1965. It was called 'The Notts and Lincs Rail Tour' and used four different locomotives. (W.Taylor coll.)

36. The box and its toilet house are seen on 9th August 1975, along with its new name which was used after Trent Power Box had been commissioned. The coal store is near the bin. (N.D.Mundy)

37. No. 58015 runs through on 1st November 1984 with open-top containers mounted on Freightliner wagons. Sadly some shelter boards had been kicked out. (A.C.Hartless)

38. Seen on the same day is the rearward view of class 120 DMU comprising coaches nos 53653, 59289 and 53717 restarting the 13.20 Crewe-Lincoln St Marks. It includes the gentlemen's conveniences on the far left and contemporary posters; also in the distance, a conveyor for sand and gravel bridges the route. There had earlier been a siding here serving Trent Gravels Ltd. (A.C.Hartless)

39. The platforms were rebuilt in 2005 and the footbridge was replaced in 2007, but its towers were retained. Our final view that day includes the 14.10 London St Pancras-Sheffield Inter City service led by power car no. 43083. This is giving us a view of the up side shelter, partially obscured by a signal support. This intrudes into the next view also. (A.C.Hartless)

40. The station is pictured facing Nottingham on 25th October 2019. Unit no. 158889 calls with the 08.36 Matlock-Newark Castle, while unit 156498 slows to collect a handful of passengers for the 08.41 Newark Castle-Matlock. The station gardens were being maintained by volunteers, two of whom are visible on the right. Annual passenger figures were around 0.1m in 2013-18. (P.D.Shannon)

The stations from here to Nottingham have further illustrations from picture 74 onwards in our *Leicester to Nottingham* album.

WEST OF ATTENBOROUGH

Chilwell Army Depot

↑ 41. The site was used for shell filling during World War I and was the location of an explosion on 1st July 1918, which killed 134 workers. The area was renamed Chetwynd Barracks and was used mainly for military vehicles until 1958. The depot was shunted by a fleet of diesel locomotives until the branch closed on 31st March 1982. On 28th August 1980, no. 228, a 1945 Drewry 0-4-0, and no. 433, a 1963 Ruston 0-6-0 Diesel Hydraulic, are seen outside the locomotive shed. The site was still in use by the Royal Engineers in 2019.
(S.A.Leleux/A.Neale coll.)

Attenborough Junction

42. The box was built in 1900 and fitted with a 30-lever frame. The machine room has just one window and the steps have a barrier on 10th June 1965, for no known reason. Closure came on 28th September 1969.
(A.F.Bullimore)

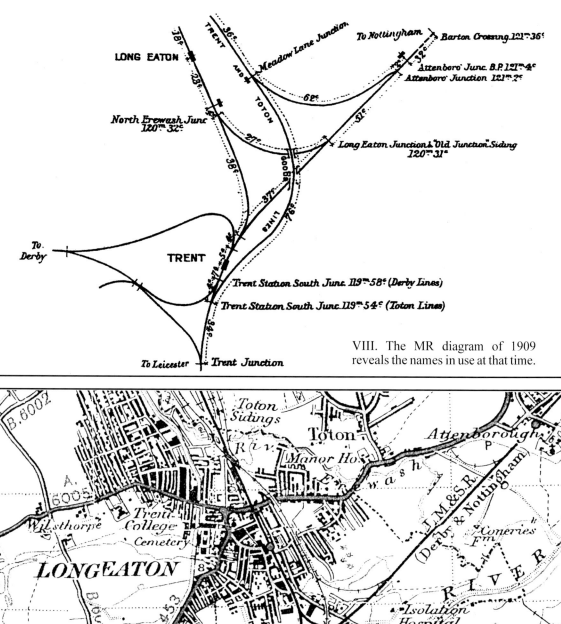

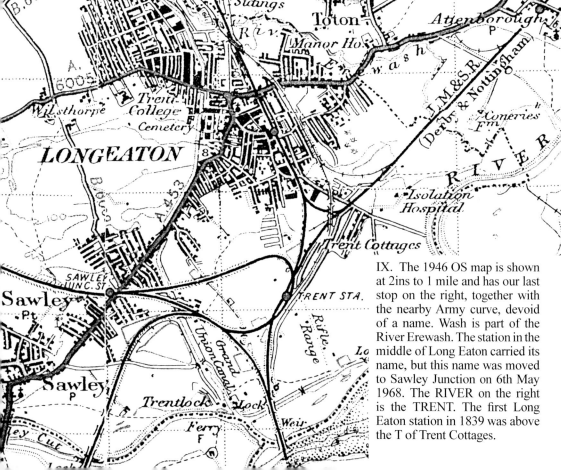

VIII. The MR diagram of 1909 reveals the names in use at that time.

IX. The 1946 OS map is shown at 2ins to 1 mile and has our last stop on the right, together with the nearby Army curve, devoid of a name. Wash is part of the River Erewash. The station in the middle of Long Eaton carried its name, but this name was moved to Sawley Junction on 6th May 1968. The RIVER on the right is the TRENT. The first Long Eaton station in 1839 was above the T of Trent Cottages.

Long Eaton Junction

43. There had been a station here from 4th June 1839 and the suffix 'Junction' was added from about 1847 until its closure on 1st May 1862. The 1893 box had 36 levers and became Meadow Lane Crossing shunting frame on 28th September 1969, closing on 16th July 1978, when Trent Power Signal Box came into use. We will continue our journey on the route of the oncoming train. (R.Humm coll.)

44. The footbridge is from where the last photograph was taken. This one and the next are from 1968. The signalman has parked his Ford Anglia close to his closet hut. (A.F.Bullimore)

45.   No. D7537 heads a batch of coal, while someone inspects the rear of the train from the bridge carrying the 1901 curve. (A.F.Bullimore)

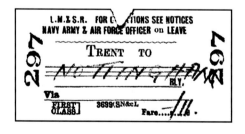

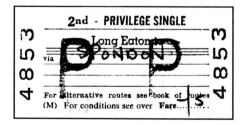

TRENT

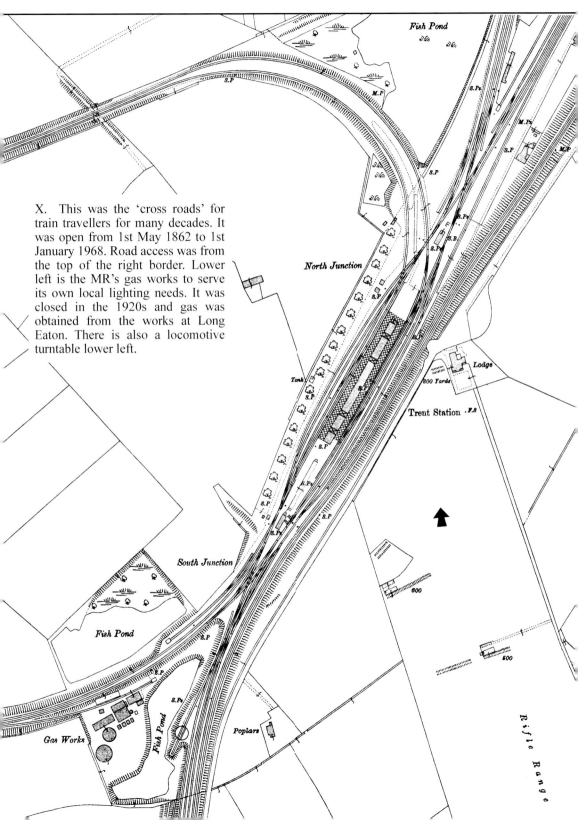

Fish Pond

X. This was the 'cross roads' for train travellers for many decades. It was open from 1st May 1862 to 1st January 1968. Road access was from the top of the right border. Lower left is the MR's gas works to serve its own local lighting needs. It was closed in the 1920s and gas was obtained from the works at Long Eaton. There is also a locomotive turntable lower left.

North Junction

Tank

Lodge

800 Yards

Trent Station · *F.8*

South Junction

Fish Pond

600

600

Fish Pond

Gas Works

Poplars

Rifle Range

46. LMS Hughes Crab 2-6-0 no. 2824 is fitted with Lenz valve gear and is entering the station from the Nottingham direction in the late 1930s. (R.S.Carpenter coll.)

47. It is 12th July 1947 and we can survey the scene in the same direction. The box is Trent Station North Junction and its 75-lever frame was in use until 28th September 1969. (R.J.Essery coll.)

➜ 48. We are at North Junction on 28th June 1952 and 1P 0-4-4T no. 58087 carries an SLS head board. It ran Derby Midland - Melbourne - Ashby - Moira Junction - Gresley - Egginton - Derby Friargate - Trent - Derby Midland. The single enormous island platform made changing trains very easy here. The path was for staff use only. (SLS coll.)

↑ 49. Rarely is the departure indicator recorded in close up. The boards are kept vertical, with names hidden from view. Three steps are built in and so even the shortest member of staff can act and also announce the details, by shouting. (Colour-Rail.com)

50. It is 1957 and no. 62568 is working from Derby to Nottingham and on to Lincoln. The 4-4-0 is of class D16/3, a type rebuilt by the LNER in 1933. The gardens were usually well-tended in the post-war period. (M.J.Stretton coll.)

51. It is 1967 and the station was still using gas lighting. It did so to its end. A little to the southwest is Trent Lock, a four-way junction on the British canal system, linking the River Soar and Erewash Canal to the River Trent, and leading to the Trent & Mersey Canal. (A.F.Bullimore)

52. This view and the next three are also from 1967. The water bag still hangs on the column as a DMU departs for Derby. Its internal glazing is still unobscured, this giving front seat passengers a marvellous vista. (A.F.Bullimore)

Trent also appears in the *Nuneation to Loughborough,* *Loughborough to Ilkeston* **and** *Leicester to Nottingham* **albums.**

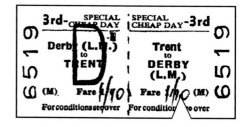

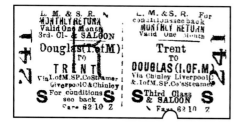

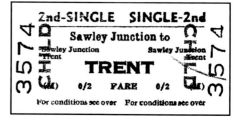

53.   A close examination of Trent Station South Box reveals the extent of the platform for window cleaners. Their water took a complex route from the gutters, through many bends in the downpipe to an open top tank, lower right. This also supplied the fire buckets, on the left. (A.F.Bullimore)

54.   The DMU is south of the station and is taking the curve for Nottingham. It bears the destination Lincoln and is close to the fogman's facility. The type of yellow panel seen in picture 52 was being enlarged throughout the fleet. (A.F.Bullimore)

55.   A final look at Trent Station North Junction box shows the rods for working the points and their access to the machine room. Herein, vertical shafts made connections to the levers. (A.F.Bullimore)

Sheet Stores Junction

56.   It is here that our route turns west to run to Derby. The box was the second one here and it opened on 1st June 1890. A larger 36-lever frame came into use on 16th March 1919. The sad structure was photographed on 23rd August 1969, five days before it closed. The Stores are shown on the next map. They were built by the MCR in 1840. The 'sheets' were tarpaulins to protect freight carried in open railway wagons, and the Sheet Stores was where they were manufactured and repaired. The original coke store building alongside the canal was converted. 230 workers helped here by 1903. Canvas sheets were sewn together and eyelets added for ropes. Next, they passed through the dressing machine that applied the waterproofing made from boiled linseed oil. Sacks were also made. An 18ins gauge internal tramway was used to move materials around the site. A branch of this passed under the main line in a subway and was connected to an additional sheet drying shed. The Stores were closed in 1963, by BR. Since then Sheet Stores began its new life as an industrial estate. (A.F.Bullimore)

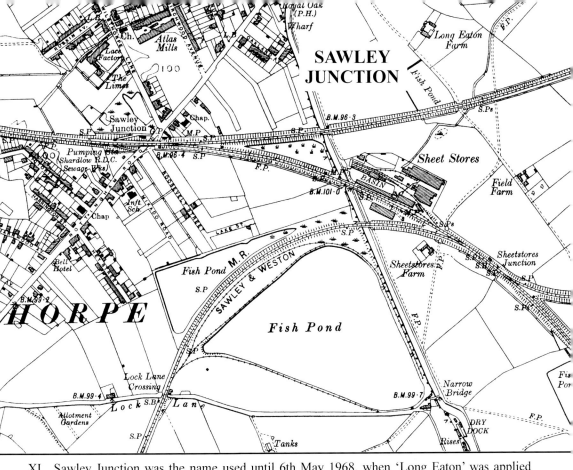

XI. Sawley Junction was the name used until 6th May 1968, when 'Long Eaton' was applied instead. 'Long Eaton' had been used for the first station northwest of Trent from 1863 to 1967, when it was closed. It is shown in our *Loughborough to Ilkeston* album. We arrive on the middle track of the three on the right of this 1921 map and find the junction shown in the last picture. Shown almost vertical on this 6ins to 1 mile map is the Grand Union Canal. The big Fish Pond has two sidings for the loading of gravel. The route curving south to Weston can be found in Section 3 of our *Nuneaton to Loughborough* album.

57.   The station is on the left of the map and its two sloping access paths are shown on it. Part of one is on the right of this view, as is the main building. Opening took place on 3rd December 1888 and the suffix 'For Long Eaton' was added on 1st January 1933. (J.Alsop coll.)

58.   Unheated shelters were provided on both platforms, plus a waiting room at road level. The signal box in the distance is shown in picture 60. This view is from about 1910. (J.Alsop coll.)

59.   A train of mixed coaching stock is seen in 1933. The LMS locomotive is 2-6-0 no. 13058. It carried this number from when built in 1927 until 1935. The raised roof on the leading coach was described as clerestory style. (Colour-Rail.com)

60. The signal box here opened in 1877 and this one followed on 19th July 1896. It was fitted with 16 levers and lasted until 29th January 1967, when it was photographed, still with its pointed finials. The small diameter chimney suggests gas heating, not coal. (A.F.Bullimore)

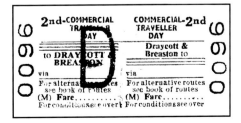

LONG EATON

61.   Passing northbound on 5th July 1975 is no. 45113, with many local observers. As mentioned earlier, the station's name had been changed on 6th May 1968. Young pupils are in train training: "It is a 1Co-Co1 from Crewe, you see." (T.Heavyside)

2nd - CHEAP SINGLE CHEAP - 2nd SINGLE Long Eaton to Long Eaton Long Eaton Nottingham (Midland) Nottingham (Midland) **NOTTINGHAM (MIDLAND)** (M) (M) For conditions see over For conditions see over	BritishRlys(M)For conditions seeBack BritishRlys(M)For conditions seeBack THIRD CLASS THIRD CLASS SINGLE SINGLE Draycott Draycott **Draycott** To **DERBY (LM)** Derby Derby 1/4½ Z FARE 1/4½ Z

62. Two views from 5th April 1982 extend our local loco logistics. Nos 20177 and 20113 pass with empty wagons bound for Toton Yard. This is at the top of map IX. They are of Bo-Bo type, which was introduced from 1957. (P.Jones)

63. We look westwards and witness no. 45134 hauling the 12.10 Derby to St Pancras. This 1Co-Co1 type was built at Crewe and Derby, weighed 135 tons and had a top speed of 90mph. (P.Jones)

64.   It is 7th November 2013 and in the modern era Long Eaton has hourly direct services to and from London. Here we see one of East Midlands Trains' fleet of Meridian diesel units, no. 222010, departing from platform 2 with the 08.25 London St Pancras to Sheffield. The prominent platform structures are entrances to the lifts which link with street level below, providing step-free access. (A.C.Hartless)

65.   In addition to the cover provided by the lifts, there are also basic shelters further along the platforms. These are seen as CrossCountry diesel unit no. 170523 arrives with the 09.19 Birmingham New Street to Nottingham, on 7th November 2013. (A.C.Hartless)

SAWLEY

66.   The first Sawley station was a mile northwest of the village on Sawley Lane, Breaston. First used in 1839, when the line opened, it was originally called Breaston, but the name was changed to avoid confusion with Beeston. It was closed on 1st December 1930. It is seen soon after that date. The first signal box was in use in 1877-96 and this 16-lever one then lasted until 29th January 1967, devoid of a gate wheel. (Stations UK)

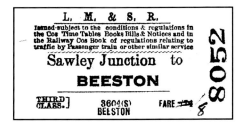

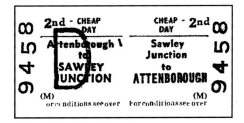

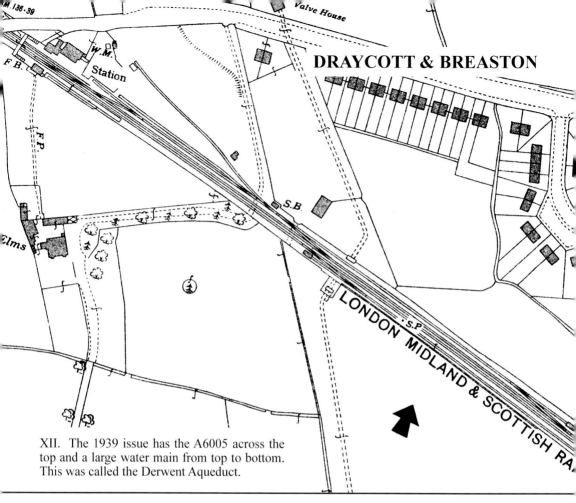

DRAYCOTT & BREASTON

XII. The 1939 issue has the A6005 across the top and a large water main from top to bottom. This was called the Derwent Aqueduct.

67. On 1st April 1852 this opened as Draycott and on 7th August 1939 it was renamed Draycott & Breaston. This view is from around 1905 and includes platform drops to aid passengers crossing. They were retained after the footbridge was built, as there was no parcel crossing provided. (J.Alsop coll.)

68. Goods trains would normally arrive on the left, uncouple the brake van and then propel the wagons over the crossover into the goods yard, on the right. The flat wagon has probably delivered some agricultural equipment. (J.Alsop coll.)

69. Just evident in this view is the inclined path link to the main road, barely visible on the map but a welcome feature for Draycott passengers arriving. (J.Alsop coll.)

DRAYCOTT STATION.

70. The engine is 3F 0-6-0 no. 43572, which was withdrawn in November 1960. Closure of the goods yard came on 5th July 1965. The yard had no crane in the 1938 listing. (Stations UK)

71. Closure to passengers came on 14th February 1966. Seats are still in place and so the date here would be prior to that. The white corners on the walls came during the blackout days of World War II. (Stations UK)

72.   The first box opened in 1873 and this 16-lever one was in use from 9th February 1891 until 28th September 1969. The disused canal from Sandiacre was infilled in 1964; this resulted in annual flooding of the track. Extensive remedial work was started late in 1996. It involved 1.5km of pipe to take the water under the line to the river and then to create a drainage ditch on the route of the infilled canal. (A.F.Bullimore)

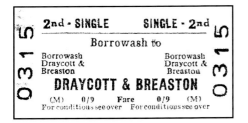

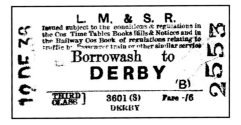

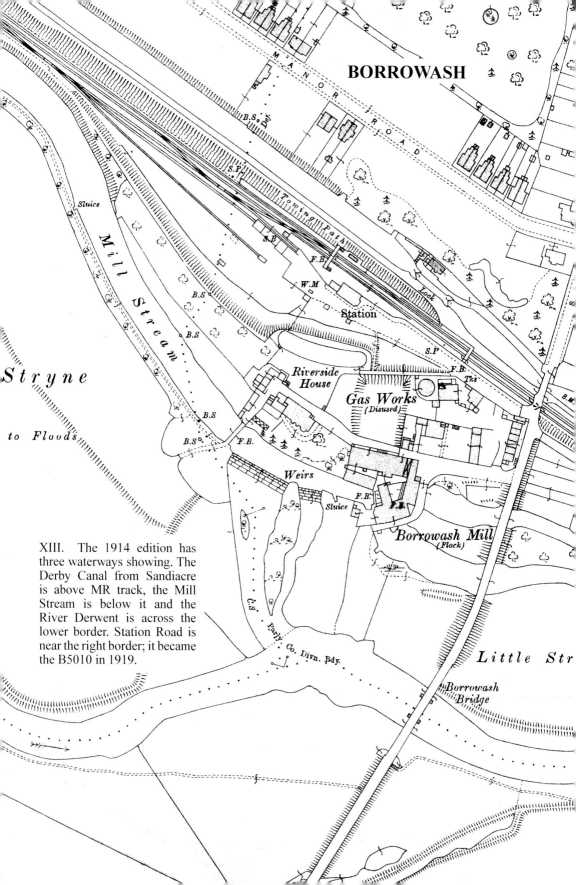

BOROWASH

Stryne

to Floods

Sluice

Mill Stream

MANOR ROAD

B.S. Wks

S.P.

Towing Path

S.B.

F.B.

W.M.

Station

Riverside House

Gas Works
(Disused)

Tks

F.B.

B.M.

S.P.

Lock

B.S.

B.S.

B.S.

B.S.

F.B.

Weirs

Sluice

F.B.

Borrowash Mill
(Flock)

C.S.

Parly.

Co. Divn. Bdy.

Little Str

Borrowash
Bridge

XIII. The 1914 edition has
three waterways showing. The
Derby Canal from Sandiacre
is above MR track, the Mill
Stream is below it and the
River Derwent is across the
lower border. Station Road is
near the right border; it became
the B5010 in 1919.

73.   The first station opened on 4th June 1839, but was a ¼ mile to the east of this one, which opened on 1st May 1871. This had the suffix & OCKBROOK from 1st May 1898 until 1st April 1904. (J.Alsop coll.)

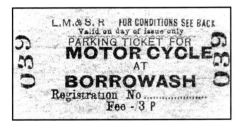

74.   This fine panorama is from the slope to the eastern footbridge, before 1914. Long frocks prevail and large sack trucks abound. The goods yard is in the background; it closed on 4th January 1965. Nearer is the signal box, which had 16 levers and was in use from 15th May 1892 to 16th June 1965. (J.Alsop coll.)

75. From a similar viewpoint in 1947, we find that little has changed, apart from the advent of cooling towers which served the power station in the lower right corner of the next map, and also map XV, before picture 91. Only their sidings are marked. The towers were demolished in 1984. (Stations UK)

76. The Power Station sidings also served Celanese Acetate in their final years of shunting. Here we witness a coal train on 7th September 1954, hauled by no. 48133, an ex-LMS 8F 2-8-0. Passenger trains ceased to call here on 14th February 1966 and the buildings were demolished in 1994, except the house for the station master at the original station site. (Milepost 92½)

SPONDON

77.   Freight is running east in about 1900 and the goods yard is to the right of the rear wagons and on the top left corner of the map. (J.Alsop coll.)

78.   Heading a Derby to Nottingham train on 1st February 1958 is no. 44414, an 0-6-0 4F. The first staff dwelling seems spacious, but only one chimney is apparent. The small glass panels enhance security. (Milepost 92½)

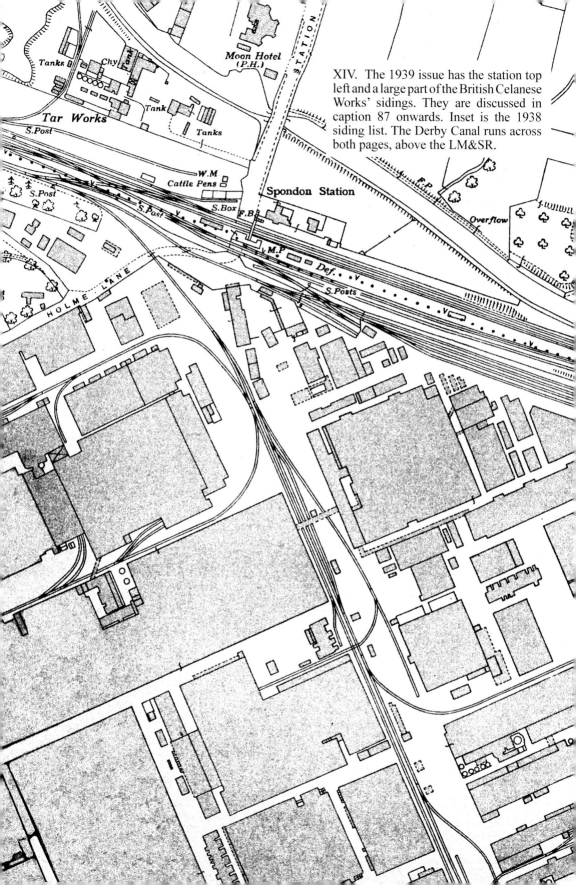

Tanks
Chy
Tank
Tar Works
Tank
Tanks
S. Post
W.M
Cattle Pens
S. Post
S. Post
S. Box
F.B.
Spondon Station
M.P
Def V
S. Posts
Moon Hotel
(P.H.)
STATION
F.P.
Overflow
HOLME LANE

XIV. The 1939 issue has the station top
left and a large part of the British Celanese
Works' sidings. They are discussed in
caption 87 onwards. Inset is the 1938
siding list. The Derby Canal runs across
both pages, above the LM&SR.

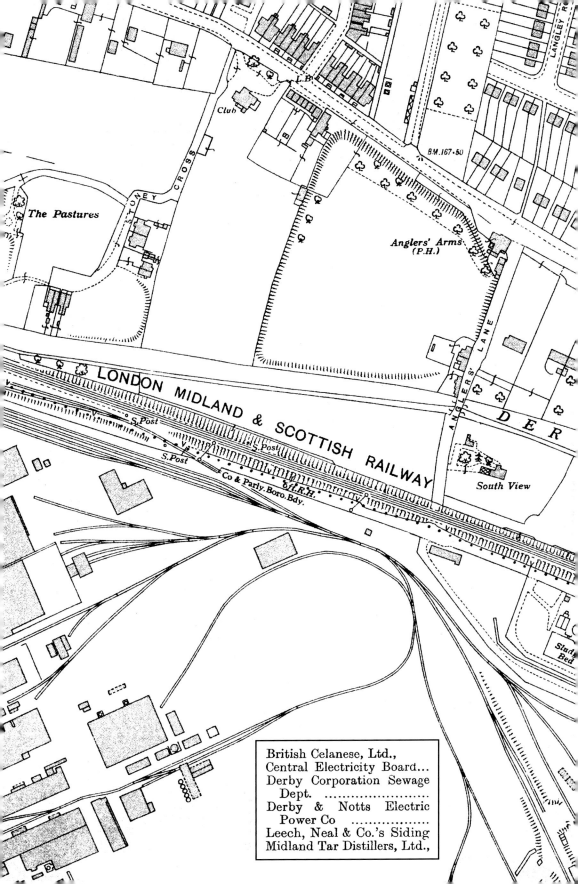

The Pastures

Club

L.B.

STONEY CROSS

BM.167·50

Anglers' Arms
(P.H.)

ANGLERS' LANE

DER

South View

LONDON MIDLAND & SCOTTISH RAILWAY

S.Post

S.Post

S.Post

Co & Parly. Boro. Bdy.

LofL.R.H.

LANGLEY R.

Stad
Bed

British Celanese, Ltd.,
Central Electricity Board...
Derby Corporation Sewage
    Dept. ....
Derby & Notts Electric
    Power Co ....
Leech, Neal & Co.'s Siding
Midland Tar Distillers, Ltd.,

79. A fine panorama from 28th June 1970 centres on the house built for the station master. Gas lights remain in use, despite the close proximity of a power station for over 40 years. The town's population was recorded as 11,541 in 1961, rising from 2550 in 1901. (M.A.King)

80. The brickwork of the old cattle dock platform survives on the right of this view from 9th August 1975, when the yard was used by a metal merchant, Albert Looms Ltd. It specialised in surplus railway material and later became a car breaker. The goods traffic had ceased here on 4th January 1965 and no record of a railway crane has been found. (N.D.Mundy)

81.   A companion photograph from the same day reveals well-maintained facilities and modern flat-bottom rail. The first signal box opened in 1876 and the second in 1889. This one opened on 26th May 1918 with 68 levers and was reduced to shunting frame status on 14th July 1969. It closed on 19th December 1988. (N.D.Mundy)

82.   With the exchange sidings for Courtaulds chemical plant visible on the left, a High Speed Train has passed Spondon level crossing and station with a service from London St Pancras on 3rd August 1984. (P.D.Shannon)

83. We are looking east from the south end of the footbridge on 31st December 1987. The two platforms on the left are in use, as is the line on the right into Courtaulds' premises. Their private sidings start at the two white gate posts. (R.J.Stewart-Smith)

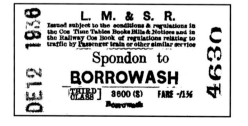

84.   Unit no. 156403 enters Spondon station forming the 08.27 Derby-Nottingham service on 25th October 2019. The footbridge is used both by railway passengers and by pedestrians wishing to cross the railway while the barriers are down. (P.D.Shannon)

85.   Despite the lack of resident staff, Spondon station was kept neat and tidy, with bicycle storage and an information point on the up platform. Unit 156405 calls with the 07.39 from Newark Castle to Matlock on 25th October 2019. Exactly 114 class 156 units were built by Metropolitan-Cammell from 1987 onwards. (P.D.Shannon)

86. Passing the site of Spondon signal box and sidings, unit no. 170102 recedes towards Derby with the 08.39 Nottingham-Birmingham New Street train, also on 25th October 2019. The rail link to Courtaulds once crossed the road on the left of the picture; the factory stopped making regular use of rail in 2002. (P.D.Shannon)

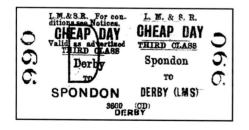

87. The Celanese Acetate production facility in Spondon dates back to 1916, when it was built to produce cellulose acetate 'dope' to waterproof the fabric-covered wings of World War I fighter aircraft. The company continued to develop in different areas and in 1921 the first celanese filament yarn was produced. In 1923 the company name was changed to British Celanese. The move into fabric and dyes continued. Acetate drape was in competition with silk, but was used widely. After decades of successful production, the company ceased operations of the flake and tow production units at the end of 2012. Demolition followed. Clarifoil, the diacetate film business of Celanese remains operational, nearby. No. 2491, built by Hawthorn Leslie in 1901, came to Spondon in around 1928 after spending its early years in Coventry. It was named *Henry* after the Chairman of British Celanese and was retired in the early 1970s and preserved; it is currently at Barrow Hill Roundhouse. This and the next picture were taken on 5th March 1966. (A.Neale coll.)

88.   *Victory* was a Peckett production in 1919, works no. 1547. In 1940, the company moved into war work again, including parachutes and underwear for the Wrens. The site was also used as an Army Storage Depot. The works employed over 20,000 people by the end of the war. (A.Neale coll.)

89.   This creation ran on 200 volts overhead wires or batteries. The locomotive was built by the English Electric Company for the Derbyshire & Nottinghamshire Electric Power Company Ltd for use at their power station at Spondon. It was one of three locos built between 1935 and 1946. They were employed to haul trains of coal from the main line yard at Spondon, along a mile long branch to the power station. The power station became part of the nationalised Central Electricity Generating Board in 1948. The CEGB sold the power station to Courtaulds. It was the end of the electric locomotive operation at Spondon. (A.J.Booth)

90. There was an expansion into chemicals and chemical derivatives. This was in addition to producing a wide range of fabrics. In May 1957 British Celanese was purchased by a competitor, Courtaulds, however the name of the works was unaltered. Further diversification into the production of vinyl acetate for emulsion paints occurred. The production of nylon-based materials grew. The company already owned a fleet of diesel shunters on the adjacent site; it was soon found more economic to use them at both sites, thus displacing the three Spondon electric locomotives. In September 1998, Courtaulds plc was acquired by Netherlands-based Akzo Nobel and the name changed to Acordis. Seen on 7th March 1991 is DL3, a four-wheeled diesel hydraulic Sentinel of 1968. It was powered by a Rolls Royce engine. The three power stations' stories are as complex as those of the chemical firms. The former supplied the latter as well as the public in different periods and used various fuels, both solid and gaseous. (P.Dunkley/Colour-Rail.com)

EAST OF DERBY

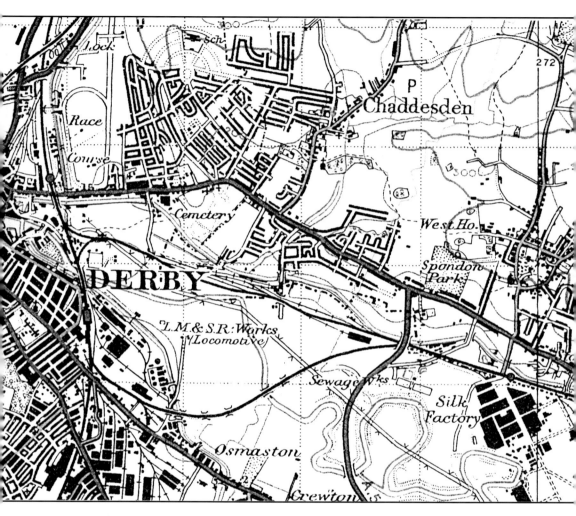

XV. Lower right on this 1946 edition at 2ins to 1 mile is a 'Silk Factory' which describes Courtaulds massive premises. The sidings to the right of them serve the power station. The station above them is Spondon. The tracks diverge at Spondon Junction, under the A5111. Thus Derby station could be entered from two directions. The upper route dates from 1839 and the lower one from 1867. The former closed in 1969. The next map shows the details west of the junction. To the right of 'DERBY' are Chaddesden Sidings. The yard's purpose was for the disposal of spent ballast and materials, reclaimed from weekend engineering possessions, which were removed from the wagons by mechanical grabbers. These worked on a ridge of ballast adjacent to the southernmost siding, depositing the spoil into large heaps which were then later loaded into lorries for distributing to the crushing facility. With only this one siding being available for the actual removal of the content of the wagons, there was much shunting required to position rakes of wagons for the grabbers to work on. When the rake was emptied, the pilot loco would shunt these wagons out into an empty road and reposition the next loaded rake for unloading.

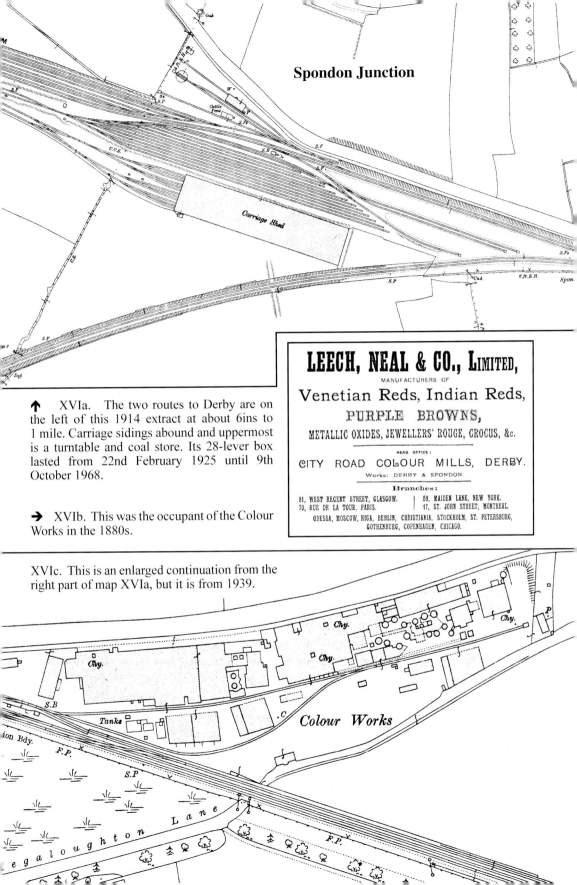

Spondon Junction

Carriage Shed

XVIa.   The two routes to Derby are on the left of this 1914 extract at about 6ins to 1 mile. Carriage sidings abound and uppermost is a turntable and coal store. Its 28-lever box lasted from 22nd February 1925 until 9th October 1968.

→   XVIb. This was the occupant of the Colour Works in the 1880s.

XVIc. This is an enlarged continuation from the right part of map XVIa, but it is from 1939.

Colour Works

91.   Spondon Junction is seen in a view eastwards, with the Colour Works and its sidings on the left. Hauling just one wagon on 14th October 1958 is 0-6-0 3F no. 43268. It is on the northern route to Derby, which closed on 18th May 1969. (R.S.Carpenter coll.)

92.   The factory is being demolished when photographed on 22rd March 1969. The first signal box lasted from 1869 to 1887. The second opened on 18th December 1887, was repositioned on 16th June 1893 and closed on 26th March 1918. This one opened on 26th March 1918, with 36 levers, and closed on 18th May 1969. The connection to Chaddesden Sidings from the east was then removed. (R.Humm coll.)

Chaddesden South Junction

93. The first box opened by 1877 and closed on 24th March 1907. No. 2 opened on 24th March 1907. A new lever frame of 55 levers was reduced to shunting frame status on 4th May 1969. It closed on 17th July 1977, and the lever frame went to Finchley Road. Chaddesden was also used as a stabling facility for weekend possession trains, with either rakes of empty spoil wagons running to possessions for loading with spoil or pre-loaded ballasts, which were usually loaded at Mountsorrel Quarry. Chaddesden Sidings No. 1 Box was the third on the site and its eight levers were not used after about 1969. No. 2 was in use in 1894-1955. (R.Humm coll.)

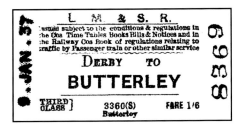

NORTH OF DERBY

Derby South Junction

94.   A 1949 view of the approach to the junction offers a rare selection of semaphores. No. 43574 is a 3F 0-6-0 and behind its tender stretch the numerous Chaddesden Sidings. (Bentley coll.)

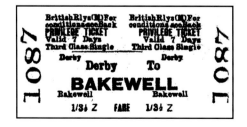

95. It is 26th March 1966 and traffic passes in the form of limestone destined for the sugar beet industry in East Anglia. No. 45043 is a class 5 4-6-0, a type introduced by the LMS in 1934. In 1960, there were 842 listed. The signalman's broom is out to dry. (Bentley coll.)

96. Situated on the north side of the curve, this was the third box here to have the confusing name, South, when it was East. It opened on 22nd May 1892; a new frame came in BR days (63 levers) and it was reduced to shunting frame status on 4th May 1969. Thus it has no signals, as evident. It was pictured in June 1969 and was closed soon after. (R.Humm coll.)

Derby Junction

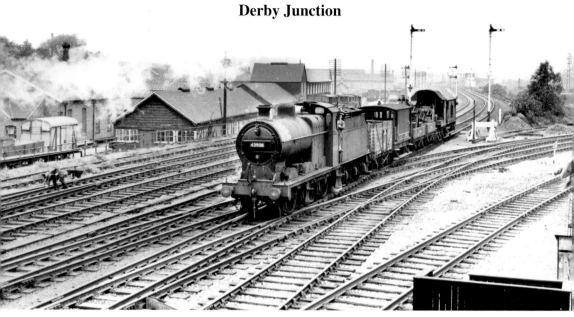

97.   On the right of this northward view is Derby North Junction. It is in the distance, along with its signal box. This had 55 levers and closed on 12th July 1969. Parts of West Junction Box are on the right; it is centre in the next picture. A breakdown train is being hauled south by 0-6-0 4F no. 43938. (M.J.Stretton coll.)

98.   Derby Station North Box is on the left of this view from 15th August 1968. The end of platform 1 and North Dock Sidings are on the left also. The River Derwent flows under the tracks, between the two signal gantries. (A.F.Bullimore)

99. We now move south of the station to see the southern 1867 approach from Spondon, which is now the one still in use. Passing the 1925 83-lever box on 4th June 1950 is 4-4-0 4P no. 41084, with the 5.35pm (Sundays only) to Nottingham. (H.C.Casserley)

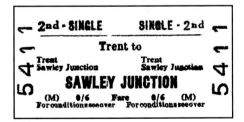

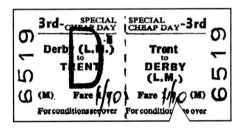

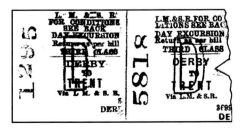

100. This is the panorama from the footbridge in the previous view, on 13th May 1955. On the right are the main lines south to Birmingham. Beyond the two gas tank wagons are the extensive engine sheds. (J.Suter coll.)

101. The bridge carrying London Road is in the background as a recently repainted DMU arrives on 15th August 1968. There appears to be a driver in training on the left of the cab. One gas lamp has avoided retirement; it must be imminent. (A.F.Bullimore)

DERBY

XVII. Scaled at 6ins to 1 mile, this 1938 extract has the two routes from Spondon over its right border. The upper one is close to the River Derwent and the lower one passes over the Derby Canal, lower right, which reaches the Derwent Foundry top left. It pre-dates the MR's foundries. The city's cathedral is further northwest. The main line to Burton-on-Trent is bottom left. The goods lines branching west from it closed on 4th January 1965. The Great Northern Railway's station at Derby Friargate was over one mile to the west and was in use from 1878 to 1964. It had stations in the northern suburbs of Nottingham.

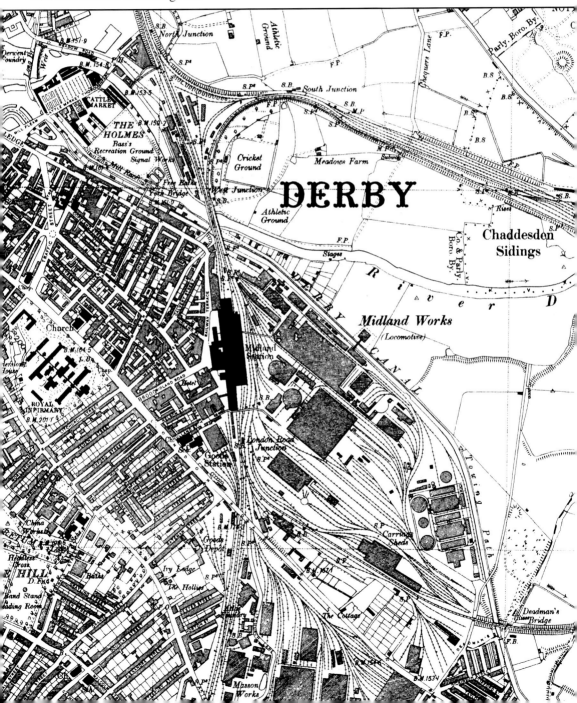

102. This drawing was created after the opening of the extensive station in 1840. There had been temporary shelters until that time. The early railwaymen were segregated by many as upper class and lower class. It was alleged that the former would talk about hunting and shooting and the latter about shunting and hooting. (A.Dudman coll.)

103. This structure was completed in 1891 and was enhanced by trams terminating here from 1904 to 1934. Trolleybuses then ran here until 1967. There are Middleton Press albums featuring both. The frontage was replaced by a modern structure in 1985. (Stations UK)

104. The 5.48pm departure to Nottingham on 26th April 1956 was hauled by class J6 0-6-0 no. 64180. This type was a GNR design introduced in 1911. Parcel traffic demanded two vans. (SLS coll.)

Hotel advertisements from *Good Lines*, monthly
journal of the Temperance Society, dated 1911.

↑   105. It is 30th August 1958 and class A5 4-6-2T no. 69820, another type conceived in 1911, has run in from Lincoln. The new building work had been completed in the previous year. The station had the suffix MIDLAND from 25th September 1950 until 5th May 1968. It had been STATION STREET from 1867 to 1906. (M.J.Stretton coll.)

↗   106. Work in 1985 saw the demolition of the historic Victorian station entrance and booking hall. The new Travel Centre officially opened on 15th January 1986. Work to demolish the canopies and erect new ones began in mid-2007 and was completed in October 2009. Numbered 156420, this two-car DMU is arriving from Nottingham on 17th May 1991. The three 8s indicate the train length stopping points. The platform numbers are 2, 3 and 4, from right to left. The National Rail award for the Large Station of the Year was won here for 2019. (T.Heavyside)

→   107. We are looking north from the south end of platform 4A at about 13.00 on 4th March 2013. On the left is an EMT 222 set; centre is a pair of 153 units waiting to leave for Crewe and, on the right, is another EMT 222 unit. The new footbridge was built in 2001 and passes to use it free were available to local residents. (P.Jones)

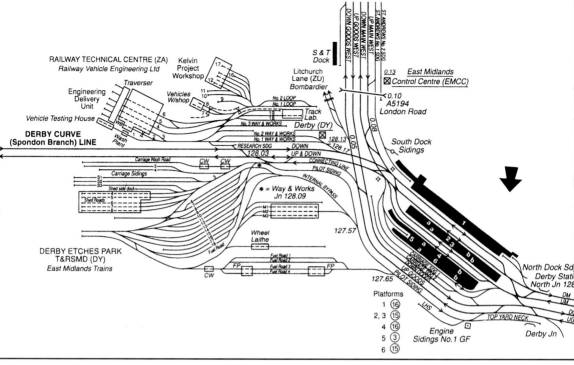

XVIII. This is the track layout in 2013 and has the route from Spondon on the left. At the top are the lines from Birmingham. The East Midlands Control Centre (top right) took over the work of Derby Power Signalbox in 2018. The new station building was adorned with the suffix MIDLAND, but only for historical reasons. (©TRACKmaps)

108. This Track Recording Train, which is entirely yellow, is seen across platforms 4 and 6 on 17th October 2015. It was a Driving Brake Standard Open coach, which was converted in 1979 from a Mark 2 Brake Open coach with a driving cab built into one end. This one, no. 9701, was taken over by Network Rail in February 2007 for use in test trains that could then be run as push-pull, and was fitted with an on-board generator to power its equipment. It was to be found in Cornwall in 2019. (V.Mitchell)

Derby Engine Shed

109. We start with two pictures from 1872. The turntable is central and the radiating sidings each contain an inspection pit. Ash removal was usually undertaken before entering the shed. The massive smoke hoods also removed unwanted steam from the domes. (J.Alsop coll.)

110. The central chimney is adjacent to the pump house. This conveyed water from the River Derwent through an underground pipe and up to the tank above the three windows in a row. There are many examples of the wagon sheets discussed in caption 56 and seen on map XI is the factory that produced them. (J.Alsop coll.)

111. The view was listed as from 1906. Nearest is 0-6-0 no. 923 and elsewhere are nos 863, 909, 2783, 442 and 87. The footbridge was for staff use only and can be found on map XVII, above the words Midland Station. It was removed in 2008. (J.Suter coll.)

112. The MR offices are in the centre background and prominent is the clock tower. Its bell had come from a chapel that was dismantled during the construction of St Pancras station. The clock was made locally. (M.J.Stretton coll.)

113. With coal dust everywhere, we find class 8F 2-8-0 no. 48083 waiting its next duty. The main roof had extensive ventilators, rather than hoods, as the tracks therein are parallel. (Colour-Rail.com)

L. M. & S. R.

Issued subject to the conditions & regulations in the Cos Time Tables Books Bills & Notices and in the Railway Cos Book of regulations relating to traffic by Passenger train or other similar service

Derby to
DUDLEY (L.M.S.)
Via Birmingham

THIRD CLASS 3360 (S) FARE
Dudley

Midland Rly. P.T.
SINGLE JOURNEY.
THIRD CLASS. THIRD CLASS.
DERBY to
LANGLEY MILL
Via Trent or Derby
FARE 4½d. FARE 4½d.
1-'28. 1-'28
Derby-Langley M (See back) Derby-Langley M

2nd · SINGLE   SINGLE · 2nd

Derby (Midland) to
Derby (Midland)   Derby (Midland)
Lincoln (St. Marks)   Lincoln (St. Marks)
LINCOLN (ST. MARKS)
Via Nottingham
(M) 6/9 Fare 6/9 (M)
For conditions see over   For conditions see over

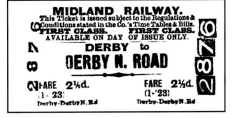

MIDLAND RAILWAY.
This Ticket is issued subject to the Regulations & Conditions stated in the Co.'s Time Tables & Bills.
FIRST CLASS. FIRST CLASS.
AVAILABLE ON DAY OF ISSUE ONLY.
DERBY to
DERBY N. ROAD
FARE 2½d. FARE 2½d.
(1-'23) (1-'23)
Derby-Derby N. Rd Derby-Derby N. Rd

Derby Works

114. The MR made most of its locomotives here, from its formation. This is another 1872 view and it has rails each side of the inspection pit. There is a buffer beam near the left one. (J.Alsop coll.)

115. This is the lifting shop on 19th July 1910. There are high rails for the travelling cranes, which could move to the far end of the shop. There is evidence of their electric motors. By 2020 the carriage works were under the ownership of Bombardier, the last railway carriage builder in the UK. (R.Humm coll.)

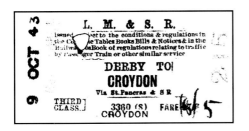

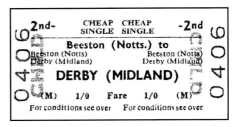

← 116. Looking east from the top of the coaling tower on 16th August 1964, we have the fields adjacent to the River Derwent in the left background and the gas works on the right. New diesels abound and the weigh house is lower right. (Colour-Rail.com)

↙ 117. A BR class 20 loco is undergoing an overhaul on 8th March 1986. This type was built by English Electric in 1957-68 and a total of 228 were made. Each weighed 73 tonnes and many were fitted with snowplough brackets. (R.J.Stewart-Smith)

↓ 118. BR Track 29 Coach/Van is on the traverser at Derby Technical Centre just after its repainting completion on 25th October 1990. The Centre is in the background. Station improvements in 2018 involved 10 signal gantries being installed, 65 new signals and 79 sets of points, plus one new platform. The original platform 5 (a bay platform accessed from the south end of the station) was removed and a new island platform constructed. The original platform 6 was renumbered as platform 5 and the faces of the new island platform were numbered 6 and 7. (R.J.Stewart-Smith)

Etches Park

119. Derby Etches Park depot dates from around the early 1960s. The facilities were refurbished and reopened on 20th May 2010 and are shown on the left of the last diagram, which is near caption no. 108. Here we witness class 158 units undergoing overnight maintenance on 23rd May 2011. The rail supports minimise pit depth. (J.Whitehouse)

➔ 120. The fleets are lined up on 23rd September 2012. On the left is no. 158813 and next is no. 222104. All are East Midlands Trains stock. The sheds cover five roads; the one on the right houses inspection facilities and the other is the main repair building. They are north of the Spondon line. (J.Whitehouse)

> **For other views of Derby, see** *Derby to Chesterfield*, *Derby to Stoke-on-Trent*, *Tamworth to Derby* **and** *Nuneaton to Loughborough* **(which includes Ashby-de-la-Zouch to Derby).**

96